Singapore

Berlitz®
Singapore

Text by J. D. Brown and Margaret Backenheimer
Updated by Wyn-Lyn Tan
Photography: Jon Davison, except pages 10, 18, 33,
    38, 44, 49, 51, 63, 64, 66, 69, 74, 106
    and 108: J. D. Brown; 4, 60, 61, 76 and
    85: Jack Hollingsworth; 89: Singapore
    Tourism Board; 30: Tony Ying
Cover Photograph by Jack Hollingsworth
Cartography by Raffaele De Gennaro
Managing Editor Tony Halliday

Third Edition 2003 (Reprinted 2004, twice) Updated 2005

CONTACTING THE EDITORS
Every effort has been made to provide accurate information in this publication, but
changes are inevitable. The publisher cannot be responsible for any resulting loss,
inconvenience or injury. We would appreciate it if readers would call our attention
to any errors or outdated information by contacting Berlitz Publishing, PO Box 7910,
London SE1 1WE, England. Fax: (44) 20 7403 0290;
e-mail: berlitz@apaguide.co.uk; www.berlitzpublishing.com

*Printed in Singapore by Insight Print Services (Pte) Ltd, 38 Joo Koon Road, Singapore
628990. Tel: (65) 6865-1600. Fax: (65) 6861-6438*

*Berlitz Trademark Reg. U.S. Patent Office and other countries. Marca Registrada.
Used under licence from the Berlitz Investment Corporation*

050/403 RP

CONTENTS

● A ☛ in the text denotes a highly recommended sight

Singapore

SINGAPORE AND ITS PEOPLE

S ingapore is a very small island nation with very large attractions and achievements. Strategically situated on the tip of the Malaysian peninsula between the Indian Ocean and the South China Sea, Singapore has made itself the busiest port in the world, the second largest oil refiner on the planet and a major international financial centre. While Singapore's astonishing wealth sets it apart from most tiny islands, it is its population that makes it unique. A melding of Chinese, Malay and Indian peoples, this Southeast Asian crossroads has become a model of ethnic and religious harmony. Singapore also stands out as the cleanest, most efficient, most highly organized society in Asia.

Yet what attracts travellers is not Singapore's wealth or its social wisdom; it is the shopping, the eating and the ethnic neighbourhoods of the island. Shopping and eating are the chief activities of Singaporeans themselves and it isn't long before visitors are swept up in these tides of delightful consumerism. Because of its special location and status as a free-trade zone, Singapore boasts good shopping for clothing, crafts, jewellery and goods manufactured in nearby Bali, Malaysia, Thailand and other handicraft centres of Southeast Asia.

> In Singapore, respect is shown to one's elders; by law, children must support their parents in retirement years.

Again, because of its location, Singapore offers the most diverse culinary experience of any Asian nation. Here, the very best Chinese, Indian, Malay and an array of other international dishes are readily available, routinely at rock-bottom prices.

Finally, for the sightseer and cultural explorer, Singapore offers historic districts to explore, from Arab Street and Little India to the Colonial District and a sprawling Chinatown. There are world-class modern attractions as well, from orchid gardens to one of the world's finest zoos. These treasures are them-selves tiny but brilliant isles in an urban sea of modern shop-ping centres (one with the world's largest fountain), government housing towers (home to millions of resi-dents) and skyscrapers (where all the money is counted).

Singaporean children out for a history lesson.

It is curious how so much (culturally, ethnically and economically) is contained in so small a space. The main island of Singapore, together with over 60 surrounding islets, covers about 685 sq km (264 sq miles) – four times smaller than Luxembourg or Rhode Island (the smallest state in the US). Yet about half of this land consists of forest reserves, marshes and other green areas.

Green Spaces

Singapore's green zones surprise many first-time visitors, at least those expecting to find a colossal air-conditioned city-state of glass and steel housed under a plastic bubble. While crowded and expanding, with a population of 4.2 million, Singapore is not the sprawling patchwork of overlapping suburbs and housing developments one encounters in many large modern cities, such as Los Angeles. Instead, Singapore can be said to be a vertical Los Angeles. More than 90 percent of its residents live in housing estates that consist of neatly kept apartment towers stretching to the sky. These residential towers are distributed across the main island in new towns, many of which have their own subway stations, shopping malls, libraries, recreational halls and other urban services. Within the tower clusters and between the towns, there are extensive green zones and areas of parkland.

Although linked to Malaysia by geography and by history, Singapore is an independent country, with a population dominated by the Chinese (78 percent). Malays make up 14 percent of Singapore's citizens, followed by Indians (7 percent). There are four official languages (English, Malay, Mandarin Chinese and Tamil), with English designated as the language of administration and Malay as the national language. In fact, most Chinese people speak a

Worshippers offer incense to the Buddhist Goddess of Mercy at the Kuan Im Thong Hood Temple.

Singapore is a successful multi-ethnic society.

variety of languages, especially Hokkien, Teochew and Cantonese, reflecting the various origins of the Singaporean Chinese.

One ethnic group that played a large part in shaping the customs, architecture and cuisine of Singapore was the Straits Chinese or Peranakans, a hybrid race that evolved from intermarriage between Chinese migrants from mainland China and native Malays. The Peranakan subculture of *babas* (men) and *nyonyas* (women) is a charming blend of Malay, Chinese and British elements. The British themselves also exerted a lasting influence on the language, customs and administration, since they literally created modern Singapore in 1819 and guided its destiny until a new self-governing constitution was approved in 1959.

Wired for Success

Singapore is a well-wired nation, with many homes linked to a countrywide network of fibre-optic cables supplying a range of services, from cable TV (40 channels) to the internet. The government's goal is to connect the whole nation to one open network, known as Singapore One (One Network for Everyone).

In Singapore's highly efficient society, transportation is a showcase of national industry. The subway (MRT) serves over one million people daily and continues to expand to all corners of the main island. The subway is quick and easy for foreigners to use. Over 18,000 taxis serve the city. Singapore's cabs are inexpensive and clean and they accept a variety of credit cards. Only about a third of Singapore's residents (who enjoy the second highest per capita income in Asia) can afford a personal car, due to the deliberate imposition of high taxes, restrictions on car use and tariffs levied on automobile ownership. This, along with other tough traffic regulations, has kept the down-

Singapore Tidbits

- Singapore's Keppel Harbour is the world's busiest port.
- Singapore supports more plant species than exist in all of North America.
- The most popular leisure activity among Singaporeans is watching TV.
- The best math students in the world attend Singapore schools.
- The Singapore Sling is still served at the place it was invented almost a century ago, the Long Bar in the Raffles Hotel.
- Nearly all (86%) of Singaporeans live in high-rise residential towers, most built by the government.
- The Suntec City mall contains the world's largest fountain.
- The lowest temperature ever recorded in Singapore was 68.9° F (19.4° C).
- Nearly 80% of Singaporeans own mobile phones.
- The number of yearly visitors is twice the total population.

town area from experiencing the gridlock and road rage common to other metropolitan areas. Singapore's airport, often hailed as the best in the world, enjoys the same unrestricted flow; clearing customs and immigration is often a matter of how fast you can walk.

Of course, Singapore's efficiency, orderliness, cleanliness and general good behaviour has come at what some critics consider a steep price. Even locals joke that Singapore is a 'fine' country,

> Singapore's leading cartoon character, *Kiasu*, is a pushy, me-first, win-at-all-costs caricature who rebels at the city's noted conformist mentality – and thus epitomizes for many the real 'hate-to-lose' Singaporean.

seeing as how the government has imposed a fine on nearly every objectionable behaviour, from not flushing public toilets to selling chewing gum. Singapore is also known as a country with severe penalties for more serious offences. Caning is still prescribed for some crimes; the death penalty is always enforced for drug smuggling. But what some Westerners perceive as an authoritarian city-state, with draconian laws and little personal freedom, is regarded by most Singaporeans as merely the common-sense way to run society. Singapore's economic success and its ability to combat such social ills as drug use, corruption and pollution have made it the envy of many emerging nations and a model for Asia in general.

For sceptical Westerners, seeing Singapore for themselves can be an eye-opener. This is certainly not an oppressed population. On the contrary, Singaporeans tend to be outgoing and cheerful, if a little competitive and aggressive. Some say that social engineering in Singapore has proved a success because it is built on the traditional Confucian and Asian values of the region. While Singapore is cosmopolitan, modern, very hardworking and Western in outlook, it is at core a society of people who place a high value on family and nation, on racial tolerance and consensus.

While few visitors might judge the politics of Singapore as oppressive, everyone could be forgiven for finding the weather so. Just 130 km (80 miles) north of the equator, Singapore is hot and humid year-round. It hardly cools off at night by more than a few degrees. The lowest temperature ever recorded in Singapore was a 'chilling' 68.9°F (19.4°C). The high humidity leaves most foreign visitors drenched in sweat shortly after hitting the streets. Fortunately, ever-ingenious Singapore has taken on the forces of the climate, too. In public areas, everything that can be air-conditioned usually is, from buses to big shopping malls and most cabs.

Instant Asia

For some, Singapore is a welcome stopover, an island of Western-style luxury with a top-rated airport that makes it the perfect gateway to Thailand, Indonesia (Bali and Java), Malaysia, Cambodia and Vietnam. For others, Singapore, with its legendary cleanliness and hygiene, its widespread use of English and its celebrated sights, shops and ethnic eateries, is a significant destination in its own right – an ideal introduction, in fact, to all of Asia.

Hindu deities on the Sri Mariamman temple roof.

A BRIEF HISTORY

With its location at the crossroads of Southeast Asia's sea-lanes, it's no surprise that Singapore has long functioned as a major trading post. Malay, Indian and Chinese merchants plied the Straits of Malacca for centuries; Chinese sailors apparently named the island Pu-luo-chung (Island at Land's End) as early as the 3rd century A.D. Malays settled the isle by the 7th century, naming it Temasek (Sea Town) and Marco Polo may have sailed by it in the late 13th century. Around the 14th century, a Sumatran prince, seeking shelter from a storm, gave the island its modern name after sighting what he thought was a lion – more likely a tiger, native to Singapore and Malaysia. Singapura is Sanskrit for Lion City and Singapore has been the Lion City ever since, regardless of the fact that no wild lions ever roamed here.

Pirates used the island as a base for centuries, as control of Singapore, the Malaysian peninsula and the Straits of Malacca wavered between Siamese and East Javan conquerors until the arrival of a man named Raffles, the founder of modern Singapore.

Raffles Rules

Sir Thomas Stamford Raffles (1781–1826) only visited Singapore briefly over a four-year period, but he left a giant's imprint on the island. An officer of the British East India Company and a colonial entrepreneur of extraordinary vision, Raffles spoke the Malay language and knew its customs. He governed Java, writing a history of the region, but his goal was to establish a trading post in strategic waters between Indonesia and Malaysia, where the Dutch, as well as the British, had considerable colonial holdings. Raffles succeeded in this aim when he landed on the banks of the Singapore

Historical Landmarks

1365 One of the earliest references to Singapore as Temasek was found in the Javanese writing *Nagarakretagam*.

14th century Singapura (Sanskrit for 'Lion City') is named by a Sumatran prince.

15th century Singapore is made part of the Malay kingdom of Melaka.

1819 Sir Thomas Stamford Raffles makes Singapore a British trading post.

1820 Chinese immigrants arrive as labourers in Singapore.

1824 Singapore is purchased by the British East India Company.

1826 Singapore is administered by the East India Company as part of Straits Settlements.

1867 Singapore becomes a British colony.

1869 Suez Canal opens and Singapore becomes an important stop along the main shipping route for rubber.

1906 China's Sun Yat Sen visits Singapore to establish a revolutionary political party.

1942 Singapore is occupied by Japanese armies and renamed Syonan (Southern Light).

1945 Japan is ousted from Singapore.

1946 The British make Singapore a Crown Colony.

1955 David Marshall heads the first elected government.

1959 Lee Kuan Yew and the People's Action Party (PAP) control the new parliament.

1963 Singapore joins the new nation of Malaysia.

1965 Singapore separates from Malaysia and becomes an independent state. Lee Kuan Yew heads the new Republic of Singapore.

1990 Goh Chok Tong takes over from Lee Kuan Yew who continues to serve as a powerful Senior Minister.

2002 The landmark Esplanade – Theatres on the Bay opens. Visitors top 7 million a year.

2003 The SARS outbreak is efficiently brought under control. The North-East Line extension of the MRT opens.

2004 Lee Hsien Loong takes over as Prime Minister.

The Sir Stamford Raffles statue and landing place.

River on January 29, 1819 and signed treaties with contending Malay sultans, thus establishing Singapore as a British trading post. The Dutch recognised the claim in 1824. In 1826, Malacca, Penang and Singapore effectively became British trading colonies under the British Straits Settlements.

Upon his arrival in 1819, Raffles found an island shrouded in dense jungle and swamp, occupied by a few Malay families and some Chinese traders. Free trade policies and firm but liberal colonial rule under Raffles' direction soon created a boomtown of 10,000 residents where 2,000 ships called annually. The sultans sold Singapore's rights to the British in 1824 and Raffles continued his social reforms (abolishing slavery), cleared the land and oversaw an ambitious construction campaign. He opened Singapore to immigration, bringing in labourers, merchants and businessmen from all over Southeast Asia, most notably from China. Raffles, in short, laid the groundwork for the vibrant free port of Singapore that remains in place today.

Raffles created colonial Singapore in astonishingly short order. He stayed only a week on his first visit in 1819, placing Colonel William Farquhar in command. He returned the same year for three weeks, devising the familiar outlines of the city, with its Colonial District on the Singapore River. When Raffles next visited three years later, he relieved Farquhar of command and oversaw the final details of Singapore's reconstruction. By the time Raffles departed Singapore for the last time, in June 1823, he had laid the cornerstone for a college that united Malaysian and European students in East-West studies. The following year, a ship fire destroyed all his writings about the region and his extensive natural history specimens. He died without heir in London in 1826, a day short of his 45th birthday.

Rubber and Tin

The British success in Singapore depended on many elements, including cooperation with the Chinese clan organisations (the *kong si*) and complicity in the opium trade, which was a major source of revenue from the 1830s onwards. Singapore became a British colony officially in 1867, just before the opening of the Suez Canal in 1869, which further spurred trade in the Straits of Malacca. In the

Chinatown shophouses, home to prosperous merchants.

first fifty years after Raffles' appearance, the island's population mushroomed from a few hundred to over 100,000. As the 20th century loomed, the export of Malaysian rubber and tin became Singapore's major industry. The pirate coves and tiger dens of earlier times were erased; rubber plantations and tin mines ruled the region.

Generations of Chinese migrants from China, many of whom married locals, came to be ardent supporters of British ways. These Straits Chinese dominated local politics and formed the wealthier ranks of the mercantile class under colonial rule, but they kept in touch with the Chinese mainland, as well. Sun Yat Sen arrived in Singapore to set up a branch of his revolutionary party in 1906.

The Great Depression in the West swept through in 1929, hurling many miners and rubber tappers into extreme poverty, but the 1920s also saw the ascent of Singapore millionaires, including Aw Boon Haw, the purveyor of Tiger Balm. Discontent with colonial rule increased in the 1930s, with the rise of India's independence movement on one side and of China's Communist Party on the other, but revolution was put on hold by the approach of the Japanese armies, bent on Asia's conquest, and by the beginnings of the Second World War.

Tiger Balm Gardens, once owned by Aw Boon Haw.

The Fall of Singapore

Winston Churchill would call the fall of Singapore to the advancing Japanese forces in 1942 'the worst disaster and the largest capitulation' in English history. Singaporeans, even today, certainly do not feel they were well protected by their colonial masters. The British, confident of an attack from the sea, had built a strong naval defense at Singapore and armed Sentosa Island to the south with large guns, but the Japanese came by land, sweeping down the Malaysian peninsula on foot and by bicycle, seizing nearby Johor Bahru. Outnumbered three to one, the Japanese nevertheless struck quickly, occupying Bukit

Standing on guard at Fort Canning.

Timah, with its food and fuel depots and bluffed the British into surrender seven days after landing on Singapore. Singapore fared poorly. Nearly 30,000 prisoners of war were incarcerated in Changi Prison, near Singapore's present airport. They were later led on a forced march through Malaysia all the way to Thailand, where many died building the railway and bridge over the River Kwai.

Residents of Singapore, especially those of Chinese ancestry, were punished even more severely than the Australian, Indian and British soldiers, since they had opposed Japan's earlier occupation of China. By the time of Japan's surrender in 1945, about 100,000 Singapore resi-

Last resting place: the Old Cemetery at Fort Canning.

dents had died through execution, or starvation.

The British resumed control after the Second World War, but their authority was now much diminished and Singapore's desire for political autonomy was strong. The British slowly relaxed their control in the region, creating a Federation of Malaya for Malaysians and making Singapore – which was predominately Chinese – a separate Crown Colony in 1955. The colony's first chief minister, David Marshall, demanded independence, but Britain would not agree. In the meantime, a new party was rising in Singapore, headed by a new leader who would shape a modern Singapore as profoundly as Raffles had shaped the colonial city-state.

Lee Kuan Yew in Charge

Singapore's modern-day Raffles was Lee Kuan Yew. Lee was born in 1923 to Straits Chinese parents, attended the college Raffles had established and then graduated from Cambridge with honours. Returning to Singapore in 1950, he cast his lot with those advocating the overthrow of the British colonialists, helping form the People's Action Party (PAP) in 1955. Supporting labour unions, working with local communists and calling for a merger with the rest of

Malaysia, the PAP won the first internal self-government elections of 1959 and Lee became Singapore's prime minister. Quickly severing his ties to communist and leftist elements, Lee concentrated on severing ties with Britain by uniting with Malaysia, Sabah and Sarawak to create the Federation of Malaysia, formed in 1963.

It was not long, however, before Singapore was being viewed as a political and ethnic threat to the new Malaysian republic. Muslim forces hastened the expulsion of Singapore, which came in 1965, dashing Lee's dream of Malaysian unity after just 23 months, but leading directly to Singapore's full independence.

Many doubted whether Singapore had the resources, the will and the genius to survive as a tiny independent nation, but Lee seemed to supply all three elements. As prime minister from 1959 to 1990, Lee has been hailed, especially in Singapore itself, as the singular architect of his nation. He harmonised the contending ethnic forces in Singapore, brought strict order to society, emphasised efficiency, embraced Western ideas, dealt harshly with his political opponents, ruled the nation like a father and focused unrelentingly on economic progress. So far, his People's Action Party

War Memorial Park: past memories and future hopes.

has not spent a single day out of office since independence and most Singaporeans venerate Lee Kuan Yew as their founding father.

The New Singapore

Under Lee Kuan Yew and his successors, Goh Chok Tong and Lee Hsien Loong, Singapore has continued to be one of Southeast Asia's brightest stars during the last three decades. The paternal approach of the government has defused racial and labour disputes, government housing schemes have provided most citizens with their own homes, and trade and business policies have attracted plenty of foreign trade and investment. While the massive modernisation of Singapore has its critics and much of old Singapore has been razed, the standard of living has risen to the highest international standards. The government's social engineering projects – which include banning smoking in public places, outlawing the sale of chewing gum, monitoring public toilets for flushing, imposing huge taxes on automobile ownership and running state-sponsored matchmaking services – have all drawn sneers from overseas, but Singapore is the most mannerly and clean of all Asian capitals (Tokyo included).

From the perspective of Western democracies, Singapore's great achievements have come at the expense of personal and political freedoms. Dissidents have been jailed or exiled, critical publications have been banned (*Asian Wall Street Journal*, 1985) or sued (*International Herald Tribune*, 1994) for unflattering coverage and the local media, from TV to newspapers, have often censored themselves into blandness. The case of David Marshall (1908–1995), one of Singapore's founding fathers, is illustrative. A Singapore-born Jew whose parents were from Iraq, Marshall was educated in Britain, became a prisoner of war when the

Japanese invaded Singapore and established himself as Singapore's best criminal defense attorney. He was elected as Singapore's first chief minister in 1955 but, with the rise of Lee Kuan Yew and the PAP, soon found himself cast in the role of dissenter. In 1969, Lee and his government banned all trials by jury, putting a severe dent in Marshall's high-profile career. Marshall was among the very few in Singapore to openly oppose caning as a punishment in minor criminal cases. The year before his death he branded Lee a fascist.

Merlion – the tourist symbol of Singapore

Such a view in Singapore today is decidedly that of the minority. Full employment, bureaucratic efficiency, social stability and a continued high standard of living have pleased most residents, who are free to vote out the ruling party under Singapore's parliamentary system. The ruling party has promised to open the political process to the people and, by making Singapore a more cultured society, stem the 'brain drain' exodus of some of its most qualified and highly educated citizens to the West. How Singapore shapes itself to fit an era of raised expectations in the 21st century remains an open question, one that may take the rise of another Stamford Raffles or Lee Kuan Yew to answer.

WHERE TO GO

Singapore can take days to explore. In addition to excellent eating and shopping, there are plenty of attractions well worth taking in. The leading sights are grouped here by district, with most located near the heart of the city and the Singapore River which flows through it. Many of the older neighbourhoods and attractions have been modernised, but there are also some areas that have escaped renewal and offer a window into old Singapore.

SINGAPORE RIVER

A good place to begin your exploration of Singapore is at **Raffles Landing Site** on the northeastern bank of the **Singapore River**. A replica (the original is found a stone's throw away) white marble statue of Sir Thomas Stamford Raffles presides by the rivershore, marking the site where the colonial founder first landed in Singapore in 1819. Flanking the statue is the new **Asian Civilisations Museum**, **Empress Place** (open Mon 1–7pm, Tues–Thurs and Sat–Sun 9am–7pm, Fri 9am–9pm; admission). Built in 1865, the stately neo-classical building once housed government offices. Today it showcases an excellent collection of artefacts documenting the civilisations of East, Southeast, South and West Asia. A smaller wing of the museum is found along Armenian Street (see page 34). The river-facing side of the building, known as **Empress Place Waterfront**, hums to a different beat at night – that of trendy restaurants and bars.

Next door to the museum is another magnificent piece of colonial architecture. The **Victoria Theatre and Concert Hall**, featuring a clock tower, used to be Singapore's old Town Hall (1862) and the Queen Victoria Memorial Hall (1905). The complex is now a venue for dance, music,

The river bank where Singapore's visionary founder, Sir Stamford Raffles, first stepped ashore in 1819.

theatre and concerts. Just in front of the building is the original bronze statue of Stamford Raffles, which dates back to Queen Victoria's Golden Jubilee Year (1887).

Behind Raffles Landing Site is a series of grand colonial buildings occupying the area Raffles designated for government offices. First is the **The Arts House**, which dates back to 1827 and first served as Singapore's courthouse. From 1965 to 1999, the building functioned as Singapore's Parliament House. Converted into a performing arts venue today, its 152-seat Chamber mainly stages music and drama performances; check <www.theartshouse.com.sg> for programme details.

Just north is the **Supreme Court**, opened in 1939, and one of Singapore's last classical edifices. It occupies the site of the legendary Hotel de L'Europe, once the city's most elegant place to stay, as Rudyard Kipling and other early travellers have attested. Next door is **City Hall**, built in ornate neoclassical style in 1929; this is where the Japanese surrendered to the British in 1945 and where Lee Kwan Yew later declared Singapore's independence from British rule in 1959.

Singapore Highlights

Singapore River Cruises (Tel: 6336-6111/9; <www.river cruise.com.sg>) ply the river down to Marina Bay daily from 9am to 10.15pm (admission), with departures from the jetties at Raffles Landing Site, Boat Quay and Riverside Point.

Singapore Art Museum (71 Bras Basah Road; Tel. 6332-3222; <www.singart.com>; admission) is one of Southeast Asia's top contemporary art galleries. Open Monday–Sunday 10am–7pm, Friday 10am–9pm (Friday 6–9pm free). Free guided tours in English available. See page 35.

Asian Civilisations Museum, Empress Place (1 Empress Place; Tel. 6332-7798; <www.nhb.gov.sg/acm>; admission) showcases artefacts from Southeast, East, South and West Asia. Open Monday 1–7pm, Tuesday–Thursday, Saturday–Sunday 9am–7pm, Friday 9am–9pm, with free guided tours in English available. See page 24.

Asian Civilisations Museum, Armenian Street (39 Armenian Street; Tel. 6332-3015; <www.nhb.gov.sg/acm>; admission) is strong on Peranakan displays. Open Monday 1–7pm, Tuesday–Thursday, Saturday–Sunday 9am–7pm, Friday 9am–9pm, with free guided tours in English at 2pm Monday, 11am and 2pm Tuesday–Friday (additional tour at 3.30pm Saturday and Sunday). See page 34.

Raffles Hotel (1 Beach Road; Tel. 6337-1886; <www.raffleshotel.com>; free) is a stately establishment and the **Raffles Hotel Museum** in its shopping arcade is stuffed with memorabilia of Southeast Asia's most famous hotel. Open 10am–7pm daily. See page 41.

Sri Mariamman Temple (244 South Bridge Road; Tel: 6223-4064; free) is the city's oldest Hindu Temple (built in 1827), where the faithful still walk on burning coals at special festivals. Open daily 7am–12pm, 6–9pm. See page 41–2.

Thian Hock Keng Temple (158 Telok Ayer Street; Tel. 6423-4616; free) is the oldest Hokkien temple and is a fine showcase of Chinese craftsmanship. Open daily 7.30am–5.30pm. See page 45.

The Sultan Mosque (3 Muscat Street; Tel: 6293-4405; free) is Arab Street's main attraction and Singapore's largest Islamic shrine. Open daily 9am–1pm, 2–4pm. See page 52.

The Malay Village (39 Geylang Serai; Tel. 6748-4700; admission) gives a taste of Malay customs, arts, history and foods. Open daily 10am–10pm. See page 57–8.

Singapore Botanic Gardens (1 Cluny Road; Tel. 6471-7361; <www.sbg.org.sg>; free) has a superb display of the flora and fauna of Southeast Asia. Open daily 5am–midnight. See page 58.

National Orchid Garden (Cluny Road; inside the Singapore Botanic Gardens; Tel. 6471-9955; admission) has the world's largest orchid display. Open daily 8.30am–7pm. See page 58.

Mandai Orchid Gardens (200 Mandai Lake Road; Tel. 6793-5480; <www.mandai.com.sg>; admission) is Singapore's largest privately owned orchid farm. Open daily 8.30am–5.30pm. See page 59.

Sentosa (Tel. 6736-8672; <www.sentosa.com.sg>; admission) is Singapore's getaway island for sun, sand and a host of other natural and man-made attractions. Open daily 7am–midnight. See page 69.

Singapore Zoo (80 Mandai Lake Road; Tel. 6269-3411; <www.zoo.com.sg>; admission) is one of the world's top zoos, employing an 'open zoo' design using concealed moats and vegetation instead of fences and concrete structures. Open daily 8.30am–6pm, it is adjacent to the Night Safari, an even larger after-dark zoo. Combination tickets are sold at the main zoo entrance for both attractions. See page 65.

Night Safari (80 Mandai Lake Road; Tel. 6269-3411; <www.nightsafari.com.sg>; admission), the world's first night zoo, employs a tram and walking trails for a fascinating close-up look at nocturnal creatures that you never normally see. Open daily from 7.30pm to midnight, it is adjacent to the Singapore Zoo, where combination tickets are sold for admission to both zoos. See page 67.

Across the street to the east of these government buildings, just north of Raffles Landing, is a large field known as the **Padang** (Malay for 'field') where Raffles planted the British flag and ordered the ground cleared. It has long been the site of cricket matches for the members-only **Singapore Cricket Club**, founded in 1852, but is best remembered as the place where the Japanese military rounded up the entire European population of Singapore for interrogation in 1942.

Even with these architectural reminders of colonial Singapore, there's little about the Singapore River area that resembles the scene Raffles and the early British traders witnessed. Gone are the mangrove swamps, sultans' palaces and the floating skulls deposited by pirates. Gone, too, are the godowns (warehouses), junks and coolies that once lined the shores. The muddy river has been cleaned up and the picturesque shophouses across the river on **Boat Quay** *(see page 31)* have been renovated and painted in pastel hues.

The massive skyscrapers on the southeast bank, in **Raffles Place**, the heart of Singapore's Central Business District, (CBD) now define modern Singapore's skyline. A handful of grand neo-Renaissance banks and office buildings remain, dwarfed by modern giants of finance such as UOB Plaza, OUB Centre and Republic Plaza (three of Singapore's tallest buildings, all attaining the maximum-permitted height of 280 m (918 ft), or about 66 storeys). Singapore's financial towers have been designed by international architects (such as I.M. Pei), but always in accordance with traditional Chinese principles of *feng shui*, which dictate the most propitious locations, shapes and decorative flourishes of the city's Western-styled high-rises.

Keep an eye out for the various public sculptures dotting the area. You'll be surprised to discover many works of art in the hustle and bustle of this commercial district, such as the bronze sculpture, 'Homage To Newton' by Salvador Dali at the foyer of UOB Plaza, or Fernando Botero's fat bronze depiction of a 'Bird' outside the building along the Singapore River. In the midst of the new urban landscape, **Lau Pa Sat Market** at Telok Ayer Street is a piece of history that remains standing. This 19th-century Victorian cast-iron structure used to be a produce market, but now houses food stalls selling local cuisine. The food outlets are lacklustre, but what's worth a stop-over are the outdoor satay stalls on Boon Tat Street just outside the market. Stands selling freshly grilled sticks of beef and chicken drenched in a spicy peanut gravy are set up in the evenings when the road is closed to vehicles.

You can board a 'bumboat' at the jetties near Raffles Landing Site, Standard Chartered bank near Raffles Place MRT, or Clarke Quay for a narrated tour of this riverside panorama of colonial and modern Singapore. The leisurely sail downstream and back passes beneath the historic

The historic Cavenagh Bridge (with Fullerton Hotel in the background) connects the civic and business districts.

Cavenagh Bridge, built of iron rails from Scotland in 1869 to connect the financial and administrative districts that Raffles had envisioned. Still open to pedestrians, the bridge now leads to the grand and lavish **Fullerton Hotel**, once the General Post Office, built in 1928. The ornate hotel, with its grand columns but a surprisingly modern interior, stands on the site of old Fort Fullerton, which guarded the entrance to Singapore from 1829 to 1873.

An underpass below the Fullerton Hotel emerges at **One Fullerton**, a gleaming new restaurant and nightlife hub overlooking the waterfront. At the north end of One Fullerton is the new **Merlion Park**, where the Merlion statue – the city's tourism mascot with the head of the proud lion and body of a fish was moved recently. Across the waters is the distinctive hedgehog-like silhouette of **Esplanade – Theatres on the Bay** (check <www.esplanade.com> for programme details and ticketing). This S$600-million centre is a realisation of Singapore's aspiration to be the performing arts hub of Asia. The massive facility houses a grand concert hall, a 2,000-seat

The distinctive facade of Esplanade – Theatres on the Bay.

theatre (both with amazing acoustics), an open-air amphitheatre, practice studios, shops and restaurants.

Riding a 'bumboat' along Singapore River will give you a view of these newest changes in Singapore's ever-changing cityscape as it passes into **Marina Bay**. Marina Bay is actually an inner harbour created by a succession of massive land-reclamation projects that include Collyer Quay and Clifford Pier to the south and **Suntec City**, a business, convention and shopping hub, and The Esplanade – Theatres on the Bay complex to the north of the river's mouth. The bumboats circle Marina Bay briefly, giving passengers a glimpse of the world's busiest port, where container ships and supertankers lie at anchor as far out as the horizon.

Successful restorations have been carried out on the quays (pronounced in Singapore as 'keys') along the Singapore River. Raffles originally ordered the creation of five quays, or embankments, created by reclamation. Collyer Quay and Raffles Quay were built south of the river's mouth; Boat Quay, Clarke Quay and Robertson Quay lined the river inland through the heart of the city. The commercial river traffic that these quays were built to service has since died out (the last river trader sailed away in 1983). Today the quays have been gracefully restored, so that you can now follow the river promenades and walkways from quay to quay, sampling what each has to offer.

Boat Quay runs on the southwest side of the river between the Cavanagh Bridge and Elgin Bridge (which was constructed in 1926 to connect the Chinese and Indian communities). It was a landfill project, built with soil removed from what is now Raffles Place, a project that Raffles oversaw personally in 1822. Boat Quay alone soon handled most of Singapore's trade. Renovation of the old shophouses and godowns was initiated in 1977 by the government, in a successful attempt to revitalise Singapore's riverside. Boat Quay has become a popular outdoor dining and drinking venue for tourists and executives from the nearby business district.

Clarke Quay, upriver from Boat Quay, on the north bank, was the site of scores of 19th-century godowns (warehouses) built by colonialists and Chinese merchants. Several of the latter became millionaires through their trading businesses at Clarke Quay. The old godowns have been restored and now serve as restaurants, pubs and shops peddling a host of merchandise and services, from fortune-telling to antiques. Across the river on Riverside Point is the **Singapore History Museum** (open Mon 1–7pm, Tues–Thurs and Sat–Sun 9am–7pm, Fri 9am–9pm; admission) in its temporary location till its original Stamford Road structure reopens after refurbishment in 2006 *(see page 35)*.

Robertson Quay is a little futher upriver than where most tourists usually venture to, but it's a pleasant shoreline walk from Clarke and Boat Quays. This former warehouse area is the largest of the three quays and is pleasantly uncrowded. The **Singapore Tyler Print Institute** is located here and houses a fine repository of international print works as well as a printmaking workshop and paper mill. In the vicinity are also trendy restaurants, cafés and the avant-garde boutique Gallery Hotel. Nearby **Mohamed Sultan Road** has become one of Singapore's hottest nightclub and bar strips, making Robertson Quay a popular haunt after dark. The river, once the very life blood of Singapore, has become a pleasant promenade, where labour and trade are forgotten.

THE CIVIC DISTRICT

For decades, visitors to downtown Singapore have referred to the area north of the lower Singapore River as the Colonial District, and for good reason. This is where many of the colo-

Preservation and Destruction

When Singapore achieved independence in 1965, the economy was in shambles. Like every developing nation, Singapore put modernisation and economic progress on the front burner; anything that stood in the way, from historic neighbourhoods to colonial architecture, was simply razed. By the 1970s, Singapore was on its way to achieving spectacular prosperity, but it had obliterated much of its irreplaceable past and visitors were beginning to complain that Singapore lacked character and colour.

By the 1980s, Singapore began to heed its critics. Historic temples, office buildings, Peranakan mansions, shophouses and godowns were more often spared demolition and restored with grace.

By the late 1980s, the government focused on four areas for conservation (Boat Quay, Little India, Kampong Glam and Chinatown). More areas have been added since. For some, these efforts at preservation come too late; for others, the preservation schemes themselves have been directed too often by commercial, rather than aesthetic, considerations.

Today's visitors must decide for themselves whether Singapore's recent conservation measures have transformed the once-gritty and vibrant colony into what approaches a Disneyesque museum, or rescued some outstanding architectural and ethnic treasures from neglect.

nial-era buildings and the museums of Singapore history stand. Raffles had staked out the north side of the river for the British colonialists from the beginning, ordering the building of offices, banks, hotels, churches and clubs there. He even built his house in what is today the Civic District, on the top of Fort Canning hill. The leading colonial architects of the time were George Coleman, who consulted with Raffles on many designs and John Bidwell, who brought neo-Renaissance plans to the Raffles Hotel, the Goodwood Park Hotel, the Victoria Theatre and many other preserved buildings. The house Coleman built for himself early on suffered the fate common to many older buildings in modern Singapore; it was demolished to make way for the Peninsula Hotel (along Coleman Street).

Fortunately, much has been spared in what has been renamed the **Civic District**, making it the most important colonial neighbourhood for travellers to stroll. The collections inside the Asian Civilisations Museum (Armenian Street) and the Singapore Art Museum are superb. The historic Armenian Church, the Cathedral of the Good Shepherd and the lovely CHIJMES complex are beautiful. The Maghain Aboth Synagogue, Fort Canning and the Raffles Hotel are major monuments to Singapore's colonial years. All lie between the Dhoby Ghaut and City Hall MRT stations, in the heart of civic Singapore.

Worth a visit is the **Asian Civilisations Museum, 39 Armenian Street** (open Mon 1–7pm, Tues–Thurs and Sat–Sun 9am–7pm, Fri 9am–9pm; admission) opened in 1997 in the renovated Tao Nan School building. Tao Nan, built in 1910, was the first Chinese Singapore school to employ the Hokkien dialect as the language of instruction. The museum's collection focuses on the unique Peranakan (also known as Straits Chinese) people of Singapore, Malaysia and Indonesia, a fascinating hybrid culture that evolved through years of inter-marriage between immigrant Chinese men and local Malay women in the late 19th century. The exhibits include displays of clothing, textiles, silver, porcelain and betel nut-chewing implements. Especially interesting are the intricate shoes and bags made of beads, a craft that Peranakan women are famous for. The main wing of the Asian Civilisations Museum, specialising in the cultures of other Asian societies is found at Empress Place *(see page 24)*.

Modern sculpture at the Singapore Art Museum.

The **Singapore History Museum** at Stamford Road is dedicated to explaining the island's past. Its impressive collection is housed in one of Singapore's most impressive colonial edifices, originally opened in 1887 (Queen Victoria's Golden Jubilee) as the Raffles Library and Museum. For the time being, visitors will have to visit its temporary location at Riverside Point *(see page 32)*. In April 2003, the museum closed for major renovations, and will reopen only in 2006. More construction is underway across the road, where the new Circle Line MRT (slated for completion by 2010) and the premises for the new Singapore Management University (SMU) are taking shape.

A short distance away, the **Singapore Art Museum** (open Mon–Sun 10am–7pm, Fri 10am–9pm; admission) at Bras Basah Road is similarly housed in a superb colonial structure, the former St. Joseph's Institution, a school set up by Catholic missionaries. The building dates back to the early 1800s, much of it designed by the French Catholic priests who presided over St. Joseph's. The museum opened its doors in 1996 and its art collection, which includes sculpture and installations as well as paintings, is contemporary, representing the works of Southeast Asia's leading modern artists. It ranks among the finest contemporary art museums in the region (past exhibitions have included works from the Guggenheim Museum in New York) and it is worth touring just to see the splendid chapel and other restored interiors.

In addition to the three national museums, the Civic District has outstanding examples of religious institutions built by the British colonials. The former Convent of the Holy Infant Jesus, known most widely by its acronym, CHIJMES (pronounced 'chimes'), may be the most beautiful architectural legacy (1860) of Christianity in old Singapore. These buildings, found within a walled enclosure at the corner of Victoria Street and North Bridge Road, have been painstakingly restored to retain their original neo-classical features, with the Gothic-style chapel, dating from 1902, standing out as the most spectacular piece. Designed by Father Nain, a French priest, it is medieval in design and ornamentation. Renamed as CHIJMES Hall it now serves aptly enough as a concert hall and a venue for weddings.

The 'Gate of Hope' entrance along Bras Basah Road was once where the destitute and desperate left newborn babies in the hope that the convent would adopt them. Today, it's no longer the impoverished who enter the convent gates, but merry-makers. The convent has been transformed into a lively nightlife hub, with the CHIJMES Fountain Court area hosting trendy restaurants (from Italian and French to

Cantonese cuisines), bars and clubs, as well as a handful of boutiques, handicraft and art shops.

Among fine churches still standing in the Civic District are the **Cathedral of the Good Shepherd** (1846), a Renaissance-style building between Queen and Victoria streets with six porticoed entrances and a high wooden ceiling, the red brick **Wesley Methodist Church** (1909) on Fort Canning Hill; the **Church of St. Peter and Paul** (1870) on Queen Street, with its original bells; and the elegant **St. Andrew's Cathedral** (1856) on St. Andrew's Road (directly above the City Hall MRT station), in the style of a Gothic abbey with its white tower, spires and commemorative wall plaques. Its premises served as an emergency hospital just before the fall of Singapore in 1942.

One of the most popular Christian shrine with visitors is the **Armenian Church** (1835) on 60 Hill Street (open Mon–Fri 9am–5pm, Sat 9am–12pm; free). It is not merely Singapore's oldest church; it is also colonial architect George Coleman's masterwork. The Armenian Church once served thousands of refugees fleeing the war between Russia and Turkey; it was constructed using the labour of Indian convicts. The churchyard contains the graves of two of Singapore's most famous Armenian residents: the Sarkies, who built Raffles Hotel and Agnes Joachim, whose

The colonial Cathedral of the Good Shepherd.

Worship at the Maghain Aboth Synagogue.

orchid (Vanda Miss Joaquim) is the national flower.

Not all of the colonials were Christian. A number of far-flung immigrants were Jewish. The **Maghain Aboth Synagogue** at 24–26 Waterloo Street, built in 1878, was Singapore's first synagogue. It remains the city's most active and in 1998 it was gazetted as a national monument. The current Jewish congregation numbers a few hundred, but at one time Waterloo Street and Middle Road teemed with Jewish households. By 1830, nine Jewish families (peddlers and dealers in spices among them) had settled in Singapore, but the Jewish population didn't swell until the 1930s, when over 2,500 Jews, mostly immigrants, were counted. At the time, it was said that the Jews owned half the rental properties in Singapore. The names of many Jewish families who helped develop the city are inscribed on the map today (Wilkie Road and Solomon Street, for example).

Further down, at 42 Waterloo Street, is **Action Theatre**, located in an old pre-war bungalow, previously a church and boarding house. Stage productions hosted here are mostly produced by young local talents (check <www.action.org.sg> for its schedule of plays). In the courtyard is a Thai restaurant, a bohemian hangout for the arty crowd and theatre-goers. Along the rest of the street are other arts centres, such as the Singapore Calligraphy Centre, Young

Musicians' Society and Dance Ensemble Singapore. At the corner with Middle Road is **Sculpture Square** (Gallery open Mon–Fri 11am–6pm; Sat–Sun 12pm–6pm; free). In the compound is also a lovely bistro that fits in nicely with the venue's old-fashioned charm.

Forming the western boundary of the Civic District and overlooking the Singapore River is **Fort Canning Park**. In Raffles' day, it was known as Forbidden Hill (Bukit Larangan), the site of a royal palace built by a Sumatran prince in 1297. Java's forces destroyed the sultans and their palaces on the hill in 1392. The ghosts of these sultans were believed to haunt the hill, the curse not broken until William Farquhar cleared the summit and erected a cannon there for defence in the early 19th century. Raffles built a bungalow on Fort Canning in 1822, occupying it for almost a year. Until Singapore surrendered in World War II, the hill was a British military command post.

Today Fort Canning has venues for drama and performing arts, the holy tomb of Sultan Iskander Shah (last ruler of pre-colonial Singapore) and nature and history trails for those seeking a green refuge from the busy downtown. The main attraction is the **Battle Box** (open daily 10am–6pm; admission), the bomb-proof bunker of 26 rooms and corridors 9 m (30 ft) underground, where British Lt-General Percival decided to surrender to the Japanese armies (15 February 1942). The bunker has been equipped with wax robots and film projections to recreate the events leading to Singapore's fall.

Other attractions at Fort Canning include a 19th-century history trail, the ASEAN **Sculpture Garden**, the original **fort gate** (1867) and a replica of the 19-ha (47-acre) **spice garden** that Raffles established in 1822 as the 'experimental and botanical garden' of colonial Singapore, and a cooking school called **at-sunrice**, which specialises in Asian cuisine.

Raffles' name is popularly preserved today in the **Raffles Hotel**, perhaps the most famous hotel in Asia. Despite the name, it was not founded by Raffles at all, but by the Sarkies brothers, Armenian immigrants who put together a small new hotel in 1886. The writer Joseph Conrad was among the first to check in, followed in 1889 by Rudyard Kipling, who praised the food but not the accommodation. The Sarkies went on an upgrade rampage (characteristic of Singapore through the centuries, it seems), adding the Tiffin Room, Palm Court and the Billiard Room by 1902. It was in the Billiard Room that the last tiger (an escapee from a nearby circus) was shot in Singapore.

Monarchs, film stars and Nobel prize-winning authors have all stayed at Raffles, including Charlie Chaplin and John Lennon. This did not protect the hotel from the neglect

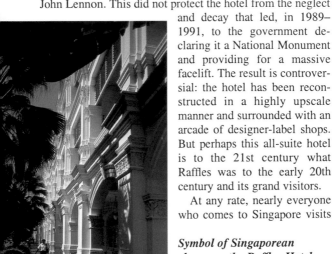

and decay that led, in 1989–1991, to the government declaring it a National Monument and providing for a massive facelift. The result is controversial: the hotel has been reconstructed in a highly upscale manner and surrounded with an arcade of designer-label shops. But perhaps this all-suite hotel is to the 21st century what Raffles was to the early 20th century and its grand visitors.

At any rate, nearly everyone who comes to Singapore visits

Symbol of Singaporean elegance: the Raffles Hotel.

the Raffles. The Bar & Billiard Room is probably the most romantic spot for a drink. The open courtyards at the rear are good for tropical dining. The **Raffles Hotel Museum** (open daily 10am–7pm) on the third floor, next to the gift shop, is small, but has an intriguing collection of colonial-era hotel artefacts. The Raffles Hotel's **Long Bar** – where the Singapore Sling was invented in the early 1900s – may be nothing like the atmospheric original (despite its ceiling fans and peanut-shells on the floor), but then, how could it be in an age of mass tourism?

CHINATOWN

Sir Thomas Stamford Raffles drew the general outlines of Singapore's Chinatown back in 1822, just after the first boat-loads of Chinese immigrants from Fujian Province landed at the mouth of the river. The Chinese found hard-labour jobs along the river; their fresh water source was a well on Spring Street; gangs, triads and opium dens became a way of life. **Chinatown**, then as now, occupied a large area immediately southwest of the Singapore River.

The Hokkien traders settled along today's Telok Ayer and Chulia streets; the Teochew fishermen congregated near Boat Quay; and the Cantonese merchants built shophouses along Pagoda and Temple streets. The tangle of provincial neighbourhoods was always confusing; Chinatown is still a labyrinth today. Visitors are almost as likely to come across a Hindu temple or Islamic mosque as a Buddhist shrine in this sprawling district (which was saved from the complete ravages of the wrecking ball only by the rise of the preservation movement in the 1980s).

A good place to begin your wanderings through the heart of the Chinatown maze is not at a Chinese site at all, but at the **Sri Mariamman Temple** on South Bridge Road,

Love Potions

Aphrodisiacs are something of a Singapore obsession. Just check out the pharmacy at the Imperial Herbal Restaurant (41 Seah Street; Tel. 6337-0491) near Raffles Hotel for a selection of the best in Chinese love potions, from deer-penis wine to seahorse tonic, which some locals drink daily. Even geckos, prolific during mating season, end up in a potent green liquor. Along Arab Street, Malay medicinal houses favour onions for prolonging sexual stamina. Indian pharmacists, relying on the Tantric traditions and the Kama Sutra, will boil asparagus and treacle in milk and ghee, spiced with liquorice. You'll find a storehouse of the ingredients used in Indian aphrodisiacs at the Mustafa Centre on Syed Alwi Road in Little India and in Chinatown any pharmacy worth its ginseng will stock a fertile line of sexual herbs, tonics and antlers to lift up a flagging libido.

between Temple and Pagoda streets. South Bridge Road was the traditional site of Cantonese merchants who specialised in herbal medicines and gold jewellery. Sri Mariamman is Singapore's oldest and most important Hindu temple, dating from 1827. The pagoda-like tower, decorated in representations of the Hindu gods, is called a *gopuram*. The interior is noted for its ceiling paintings and the temple is the site for the Thimithi ceremony in which believers walk on burning coals.

A stroll down Temple Street (off South Bridge Street) takes one past plenty of Chinese souvenir shops (lacquerware, silks, Tiger Balm ointments) to Trengganu Street, now an outdoor street vendors' mall, but previously an opera street with theatre stages and houses of prostitution. On the left is Smith Street, a re-created alley of open-air hawker stalls that's reminiscent of the old days. Trengganu Street terminates at Sago Street, another colourful shopping area with its Chinese pharmacies, rattan weavers, kite-makers, pastry shops and carpenters. Just off Sago Street is Banda Street, the best place to shop these days for paper offerings meant to be burned at funerals. The offerings, which come in the shapes of Rolls Royces, laptop computers, mobile phones and credit cards, as well as cash, are sent heavenward in smoke to the deceased, who apparently have not renounced consumerism in the afterlife.

Temple Street and the parallel Pagoda Street both lead westward in short order to New Bridge Road and Eu Tong Sen Street, where the new Chinatown MRT station opened in July 2003. Worth a detour at 48 Pagoda Street is the interesting **Chinatown Heritage Centre** (open Mon–Thurs 9am–8pm, Fri–Sun 9am–9pm; admission). The Centre showcases Chinatown's rich cultural heritage, and includes a recreation of the cramped living conditions of the early Chinatown residents.

Eu Tong Sen Street is the location of several of Chinatown's most interesting and gritty shopping arcades (People's Park Complex and People's Park Centre, with its textile dealers), and the Yue Hwa Department Store with its Chinese clothes and souvenirs.

The Sri Mariamman Temple: ritual bathing.

Club Street shophouse turned into a nightclub.

Most of Chinatown's attractions, however, lie east of South Bridge Road.

Ann Siang Road and **Club Street**, once the haunt of letter-writers for hire, are filled with finely restored shophouses (as well as a few colourful unrestored specimens). The style is not entirely Chinese. The carved decorations and swinging 'cowboy doors' are Malay in origin, while the Georgian windows and art deco touches are European. The tiled roofs are strictly Chinese, of course. True to its name, Club Street was once home to trade associations, but is now a dining hub with trendy bars and restaurants housed in the restored shophouses. Choose from a cosmopolitan array of cuisine, from Chinese to French and fusion.

Club Street rises and plunges into Upper Cross Street, the location of **Far East Square**, **China Square Food Centre** and **China Square Central**, three large food and entertainment centres that replaced the traditional food and shopping streets many Singapore Chinese grew up with. Far East Square is worth a stroll for its interesting shophouses and entrance gates which represent the five elements that make up the Chinese universe. On the east side of Far East Square is Telok Ayer Street, worth strolling for its cluster of national monuments, beginning with the **Fuk Tak Chi Museum** (open daily 10am–10pm; free). The museum, with both original and restored pieces of the old 1824 temple complex, reopened in 1998 when the area was urbanised. Further along Telok Ayer Street are three places of worship. First up is the **Nagore Durgha Shrine**, built between 1828–30 by Muslims from Southern India. The tiny mosque is hidden by hoarding and is currently closed for renovation.

Adjacent to it is **Telok Ayer Green**, a tiny park that's both restful and informative, with shaded seats and life-sized bronze figurines depicting scenes from the past. Next is the **Thian Hock Keng Temple** (Temple of Heavenly Bliss), built between 1839 and 1842, which traces its origins to the first Chinese immigrants, who built this elaborate Taoist shrine to their maritime protector, Ma Chu Poh, the Goddess of the Sea. Recently restored, it employs granite pillars from south China, blue tiles from Holland and cast-iron railings from Scotland. Although the main altar is Taoist, a rear chamber dedicated to Guanyin, Goddess of Mercy, is Buddhist. Before reclamation, this temple stood on the edge

Chinese pharmacies sell everything from tea to powders
purporting to have aphrodisiacal qualities.

of the sea. The last temple on Telok Ayer Street is **Al-Abrar Mosque**, known as the Indian (or Chulia) Mosque, which opened in 1855. Singapore's remarkable mingling of ethnic and religious groups is quite visible in the consecutive placement of these three diverse places of worship, although only the Thian Hock Keng Temple receives visitors regularly.

There are still many sights in Chinatown just off the main tourist routes. The **Eu Yan Sang Medical Hall** (269 South Bridge Road; open Mon–Sat 9am–1pm, 2–6pm), which opened in 1910, is the ultimate Chinese pharmacy. Here visitors can sample or purchase everything from ginseng tea to wines purported to have aphrodisiacal qualities.

The **Tanjong Pagar Conservation District**, at the south end of South Bridge Road, is another area of similarly restored shophouses, the popular **Maxwell Food Centre** and, more recently, **The Scarlet**, a swanky new boutique hotel at 33 Erskine Road. Step in, if only to gawk at the dramatic interiors and browse the adjoining speciality shops and galleries. The **Singapore City Gallery** (open Mon–Fri 9am–5pm, Sat 9am–1pm; free) in **The URA Centre** nearby is an informative stopover with its interactive exhibits on Singapore's city

Prayers at Thian Hock Keng Temple (the Temple of Heavenly Bliss), built by the first Chinese immigrants.

planning. Over 200 shophouses have been meticulously restored along Neil Road, Murray Terrace, Craig Road and Duxton Hill Road.

LITTLE INDIA

Among the first Indian settlers were 120 assistants and soldiers who sailed into Singapore in 1819 with Raffles. They lived in Chinatown along Chulia Street, the original Indian quarter, but as cattle-raising increased along the Rochor River to the north, India's immigrants congregated in an area bisected by Serangoon Road which is now known as **Little India**. Hindus are in the majority here

Shop for a stylish sari in Little India.

among Indians, although Tamil Muslims are well-represented; both groups, however, are dominated numerically by Chinese, who make up almost three-quarters of Little India's population. This is perhaps the most colourful downtown neighbourhood to stroll in Singapore, its back streets and thoroughfares marked with the 'five-foot ways', or covered corridors, that arch out from the shophouses.

For a walking tour of Little India, start at the **Little India Arcade** on Serangoon Road, opposite the Tekka Centre (a market and vendors' emporium). The Little India MRT station nearby opened in July 2003, making it even easier to get here. The arcade, converted from shophouses in 1982, has a 'cultural corner' with period photographs of Serangoon Road and illustrations of the food, fashions and customs of Singapore's Indian community, most of whom first immigrated from the Calcutta and Madras in South

Hindu devotee at the Sri Veeramakaliamman temple.

India. The Little India Arcade has shops selling *saris* (colourful wraps) and *cholis* (short-waisted blouses), as well as sweets, medicines, betel nuts, carvings and brassware. There's also a food centre inside, where you can dine cheaply on a variety of Indian dishes. Sadly, even Little India has not been spared from urbanisation. Next door is the new (and ugly) six-storey **Tekka Mall** housing even more shops and restaurants.

From the Little India Arcade you can wander north up Serangoon Road, exploring the flavourful side streets as they come. Campbell Lane is filled with five-foot ways and shops selling woodcarvings, furniture and musical instruments. Dunlop Street has textile and dress shops, as well as small, exotic groceries. A few blocks down at 41 Dunlop Street (near the Perak Street junction) is the **Abdul Gaffoor Mosque**. Most Singaporean Indians are Hindu, but the Muslim faithful congregate here on Fridays. The mosque (except for the prayer hall) can be visited if you dress respectfully (with your legs covered). Dating from 1859, the present brick structure, blending Arabic and European styles, opened in 1907. A block north, on 25G Perak Road, is the **Church of the True Light**, an Anglican place of worship built in 1952 to serve the needs of Little India's Chinese Christian residents.

Returning to Serangoon Road, famous for its goldsmiths, you can take a brief detour down Cuff Road for a look at the **Spice Grinder Shop** (open Mon–Sat 8am–1pm, 2–5pm), a noisy, but fragrant enterprise, one of the last remaining in Singapore, where the freshest mixes of spices, flours and betel nuts are custom-ground. A little farther up Serangoon Road, at Belilios Road, is the **Sri Veeramakaliamman Temple**, constructed by Bengalis in 1855. This is one of Singapore's finest Hindu shrines.

Dedicated to Kali, the Hindu Goddess of Power, it is packed with fervent followers on the Hindu holy days – Tuesdays and Fridays. Visitors are free to enter this temple, which is noted for its coconut-cracking custom. Devotees often break a coconut before entering to denote the breaking of their ego. Cracked shells are tossed into the aluminum receptacles under the *gopuram* (sculptured gate tower). This temple interior is fascinating for the number of Hindu symbols it employs. Fresh coconut and mango leaves above the entrance are for purity and welcome; the lotus represents human striving for spiritual perfection; banana offerings indicate abundance.

A good way north up near Farrer Park MRT, at 397 Serangoon Road, is another national monument: the **Sri Srinivasa Perumal Temple**, dating from 1855, has a vast prayer hall to

Cracked coconuts symbolise the surrender of selfish ways.

honour Krishna (also known as Perumal), one of the incarnations of Vishnu, the supreme Hindu god. The temple is topped by a five-tier *gopuram* tower, donated by P. Govindasamy Pillai, an early Indian migrant made good.

Nearby, at 366 Race Course Road, which runs parallel to the west of Serangoon Road, is the **Sakya Muni Buddha Gaya Temple**, better known as the **Temple of 1,000 Lights**. This Buddhist shrine, maintained by Thai monks, is one of the most popular religious shrines in Singapore. Its centrepiece is the seated Buddha statue, 15 m (49 ft) tall and weighing in at 305 kg (300 tons). The Buddha is surrounded by light bulbs that light up every time a donation is made. The scene is spectacular, if kitsch, complete with several Hindu statues and two bright yellow tigers posted as guards outside.

The temple across the road, at 371 Race Course Road, is **Leong San Buddhist Temple** (Dragon Mountain Temple), a less fanciful place of Chinese worship. It's a Taoist shrine, dedicated to the Goddess of Mercy, Guanyin. Ancestral tablets are stored at the back and there's a prominent statue of Confucius here – who was neither Taoist nor Buddhist, Hindu nor Muslim.

Farther still up Serangoon Road, at 2 Towner Road, is the **Central Sikh Temple**, a formidable modern concrete structure with a dining hall on the first floor and a domed prayer hall on the second floor, where Sikhs go to pray under the cool fans during the heat of the day. Colourful wall posters recount the history and principles of the Sikh religion.

KAMPONG GLAM

Named after the gelam trees that once grew here, the **Kampong Glam** district (north of the Civic District and the Singapore River) was the historic seat of the Sultans. Settled by Muslims from Malaysia and the Buginese from

When the Spirit Moves You

Mediums, who channel messages from the afterlife while in a trance, are surprisingly common in Singapore. They operate in small temples and in their own medium houses, which resemble rundown Taoist temples. Many, if not most, Singaporeans seem to believe in their power. Mediums are frequently called upon to forecast upcoming lottery numbers. Their trances are flamboyant. Mediums often gyrate rapturously, swoon, fall and dash from point to point. Piercings are nearly mandatory. Long needles are inserted through elbows, wrists, hands, mouths, or tongues, to be withdrawn as the trance abates, usually leaving no blood or visible wound. Two temples, both west of Chinatown off Zion Road, where you're most likely to see a medium at work are the small **Giok Hong**

Tian Temple (Temple of the Heavenly God) at Zion and Havelock roads, a Taoist shrine where throngs of worshippers take a joss stick home with them on New Year's Day for good fortune and the **Monkey God Temple (Tse Tien Tai Seng Yeh)**, at the corner of Eng Hoon Street and Tiong Poh Road, a family shrine that has grown as the temple medium's flock has grown. On the Monkey God's birthday in the fall, a number of mediums congregate at the Monkey God Temple, pierce themselves and enter into sustained, dramatic trances.

Indonesia, this neighbourhood has maintained a pronounced Islamic character, especially around Arab Street.

☛ **Arab Street** is the traditional home of Singapore's textile dealers and there are still many small silk and batik stores here, as well as sarong shops. Leather goods, caneware, fishing gear and shiny metalwork are also for sale in the shophouses and make for an interesting browse. Come early, as most shops close after 5pm. **Kazura Perfume Shop** at 51 Haji Lane has a fine display of decanters; the perfumes are non-alcoholic versions of Western standards.

☛ The leading attraction is the **Sultan Mosque**, located between Arab Street and North Bridge Road at the end of Bussorah Street. It's an impressive edifice with its massive onion-shaped golden dome and corner minarets. A National Monument that dates back to 1825, this is Singapore's largest mosque; visitors are welcome to observe (but not enter) its grand prayer hall. Next door is the **Malay Heritage Centre** (open Mon 1–6pm, Tues–Sun 10am–6pm; admission. Compound open daily 9am–9pm; free). The Centre is housed in the compound of **Istana Kampong Gelam**, which was the former residence of the son of the first Sultan of Singapore, and dates back to the 1840s.

At 44 Kandahar Street is **Bumbu** (Tel. 6392-8628), an Indonesian restaurant filled with an eclectic collection of rare antiques sourced from various Singaporean homes. You could glimpse an interesting insight into Singapore's multicultural heritage here. At the corner of Jalan Sultan and Victoria Street is the **Malabar Jamah-Ath Mosque**, famous for its blue tile work. Northeast of the Sultan Mosque, at 4001 Beach Road, is the **Hajjah Fatimah Mosque**, built in 1846 by the Malaysian wife of a Bugis merchant as a private residence. Its remarkable architecture mixes European and Chinese influences with a Malaysian minaret that resembles the white spire of a cathedral. The minaret is off the plumb, leading some to dub it 'the leaning tower of Singapore'.

Bugis Street, south of the Arab Street area on Victoria Street, was Singapore's most notorious after-dark hangout until it was razed in 1985 to construct the Bugis MRT station. Now, in place of a street internationally renowned for prostitution and drag queens, there is **Parco Bugis Junction**, a glitzy shopping mall with a glassed-over air-conditioned shopping street and the adjoining luxury Hotel Inter-Continental. Across Victoria Street from the MRT station is a street market that comes alive at night. It's slightly reminiscent of Bangkok's Chatuchak market in the sense that it's hot, crammed and crowded. There are some value finds here, like look-alike Oakleys and cheap, fashionable streetwear, but locals and tourists mostly come here to soak in the atmosphere and haggle for copy VCDs and cheap souvenirs.

What is worth seeing in the Bugis neighbourhood are the two shrines two blocks to the west on Waterloo Street. The **Kuan Im Thong Hood Temple** is one of the most crowded

Little India street stalls sell garlands of scented flowers in colours that symbolise purity, happiness and prosperity.

Temple to consumerism: Orchard Road shopping mall.

in the city. The Buddhist Goddess of Mercy, Guanyin, presides here. Rebuilt in 1982, the temple architecture is not the attraction – rather, it is the flower-sellers outside as well as the supplicants inside. This is a fine opportunity to watch worshippers offer incense and flowers to the goddess, kneel and shake fortune sticks in a box, then consult with the priests as to the meaning of the stick that first appears. From lottery numbers to the prospects for offspring, the goddess tries to unravel the future from 6am to 6.15pm daily. Just next door, at 152 Waterloo Place, is a Hindu shrine, the **Sri Krishnan Temple**, highly ornamented, with incense sticks out front for the convenience of worshippers who spill over from next door.

ORCHARD ROAD

Orchard Road, running west from the Civic District and Dhoby Ghaut MRT station, is Singapore's best known shopping avenue and dining district, though it has some sights worth seeing, too. The name of this glitzy road goes back to the 1840s, when Captain William Scott established his nutmeg and pepper plantation on the slopes. Tigers roamed the hills along Orchard Road until 1846; fifty years later, the land was tamed and some of Singapore's richest families had built their estates and terrace homes here.

The most notable cluster of these historic residences is on **Emerald Hill**, the site of one of Singapore's first and most impressive preservation projects. A stroll up Emerald Hill Road from Peranakan Place is a walk into Singapore's stately colonial past. The terrace houses were constructed between

Orchard Road Rejuvenation Effort

In a bid to double tourist arrivals and triple tourism revenue, the Singapore Tourism Board (STB) has put into motion major plans to transform the Orchard Road retail area into one of the world's best shopping and events venues. To achieve this end, premier sites in the district will be released for the development of multi-concept lifestyle establishments comprising retail, food and beverage, and entertainment facilities. In particular, two areas above the Orchard MRT station and the Somerset MRT station are being earmarked for major anchor retail development.

Plans also include the enhancement of street infrastructure and landscape; the relaxation of building guidelines to allow for more dynamic building facades and larger shopping space; and the improvement of traffic and pedestrian flow, all of which aim to make shopping a safer and more varied experience. Specially designated space for youth activities and community events, as well as for cultural exhibitions, will also be incorporated to inject vibrancy and excitement into the area. The entire rejuvenation effort will cost both the private and public sectors some S$2 billion.

1902 and 1930 on the site of a nutmeg farm by a variety of architects using a plethora of Malay, Chinese and European styles. The original owners were wealthy Peranakan, a mixed race that evolved through intermarriage between immigrant Chinese men and local Malay women in the 19th century. Pastel hues, fancy plaster work, ornate grills, shuttered windows, bat-shaped openings, tiled overhangs and carved wood characterise many of these graceful exteriors. There are a few galleries and restaurants among the houses, which allows a glimpse of their colonial-period interiors, but most of the restored terrace homes and shophouses are expensive private residences. The carved door-fences (*pintu pagar*) are designed for ventilation and privacy.

Orchard Road is also the address of the **Istana**, the palace that is home to Singapore's president. Indian convicts did the heavy work on this government estate in the late 1860s, which is unfortunately closed to visitors except on Chinese New Year's Day, Hari Raya Puasa, Labour Day, Deepavali and National Day. If you are there on the first Sunday of any month, you can catch the changing of the guard at the Istana gates (starting at 6pm). Further away but more accessible is the **Goodwood Park Hotel** at 22 Scotts Road, a national landmark built in 1900 as the Teutonia Club for German colonialists. The Goodwood vies with the Raffles as Singapore's most luxurious historic hotel. Resembling a Rhineland castle with its eight-sided Bavarian tower, it was occupied by Japanese officers during the war, serving as the War Crimes Court later. Celebrities who have spent the night here include Anna Pavlova and John Wayne.

On the south side of Orchard Road (west of Fort Canning) are three religious sites. The **Chesed-El Synagogue**, less active than Maghain Aboth Synagogue on Waterloo Street *(see page 38)*, opened in 1905 on Oxley Rise. It served as the private synagogue for Menasseh Meyer, a real-estate tycoon. **Chettiar Temple** on 15 Tank Road, also called Sri Thandayuthapani, was rebuilt in 1884. It was traditionally the temple favoured by the Hindu *chettiar* community, Indian money-lenders from Madras. The temple's *gopuram* (tower) is one of the most lavishly carved pantheons of Hindu gods in Singapore. The interior is equally ornate. The annual Thaipusam Festival procession from the Sri Srinivasa Perumal Temple *(see page 94)* ends here, with coconuts, symbolising the ego, smashed open on the courtyard pavement.

Hindu god at Chettiar Temple

GEYLANG SERAI

When the British transformed Singapore into a trading colony, many Malays took up residence in **Geylang Serai**, east of the city centre. The district still has a strong Malay character, complete with old bungalows, terrace houses and Peranakan shophouses, especially along Joo Chiat and Koon Seng roads near the Paya Lebar MRT station. Singapore's largest red-light district and a cluster of 'love hotels' are located in the *lorong* (alleys) here. So, too, is the **Geylang Serai Market** near Geylang Road, selling fish, fruit and clothing. Across from the market is the **Malay Village** (open daily 10am–10pm; free), a theme park re-creation of *kampong* (village) stilt-house architecture, with cafés and cultural shows. There is a museum in the village featuring a fine display of Malay wedding customs. This is a good place to see demonstrations of kite-making, batik work and kampong games.

ZOOS, PARKS AND ORCHID GARDENS

Some of Singapore's top attractions lie outside the crowded urbanised centres and neighbourhoods of downtown Singapore. These include the island's world-renowned zoos, a park devoted to birds, nature reserves and the orchid farms which form a much appreciated counterweight to the city-state's metropolitan-laden landscape.

The **Singapore Botanic Gardens** (open daily 5am–midnight; free) on Cluny Road, just west of Orchard Road, is the nearest major green preserve to the downtown district. The 52-ha (128-acre) site of gardens and jungle forests was opened in 1859 as a repository of Southeast Asian flora and fauna. The gardens begin at Swan Lake, surrounded by palms and rubber trees, then lead past an 1860 bandstand and a topiary garden. A new 1.5-ha (3.7-acre) **Evolution Garden**

Singapore's Botanic Gardens are packed with colour.

traces life on earth from 4,600 million years ago till the present day with live exhibits and plant replicas. A must-visit is the **National Orchid Garden** (open daily 8.30am–7pm; admission), which claims to have the world's largest display of Singapore's signature bloom. It has over 3,000 varieties of orchids, including an ample display of Singapore's national flower, the purple Vanda Miss Joaquim – first discovered in 1893 by an Armenian immigrant, Agnes Joachim. A visit here includes a glimpse of the VIP orchids, named after the dozens of female dignitaries who have visited Singapore. Located within this garden is the newly-opened **Cool House**, which encloses a montane tropical forest.

Singapore's most often-visited flower farm is the **Mandai Orchid Gardens** (open daily 8.30am–5pm; Tel. 6793-5480; admission) on 200 Mandai Lake Road, well north of the downtown area, near the zoo. Operated by a private grower, the Mandai Orchid Gardens exports cut flowers and plants to over 30 countries worldwide. The water garden includes tropical plants from many countries that do well in Singapore's climate, including heliconia and traveller's palm. Gardeners are usually hard at work tending the orchids, which require intensive cultivation.

Another alternative for orchid-fanciers is **Orchidville** (10 Lorong Lada Hitam; open Sun–Fri 8am–5pm, Sat 8am–10.30pm, public holidays 8am–3pm; Tel. 6552-7003; free), also located on Mandai Road, opened in 1993 by the Phua family, who had been successful pig farmers in the past. Their greenhouse approach to creating a humid environment for growing orchids seems to have paid off, extending the lives of their blooms. Visitors are welcome to view some of the two million pots of orchids; visitors can also cut their own flowers to take home or arrange overseas shipping of purchases. Each pot has a life expectancy of five years. Some

Ornate pavilion at Chinese Garden.

400,000 new plants are bred each year to maintain the stock, and this makes the enterprise the largest in Singapore.

Gardens of a different order are maintained at the **Chinese and Japanese Gardens** (1 Chinese Garden Road; main gate open daily 6am–11pm; free; Bonsai Garden and Garden of Abundance open daily 9am–6pm; admission). The Chinese garden reflects several classical styles and employs twin pagodas, arched bridges, an extensive *bonsai* display, elaborate rock works, a teahouse and even a marble boat like the one in Beijing's Summer Palace gardens. From the Chinese Garden visitors cross a bridge into the Japanese Garden with its carefully raked Zen rock gardens, stone lanterns, pavilions and pools. They have a quiet, almost desolate look, but they are crowded during Chinese New Year and the Lantern Festival.

Far more lively, but also fallen on hard times lately, is the most Chinese of Singapore's theme parks, **Haw Par Villa**, also known as **Tiger Balm Gardens** (262 Pasir Panjang Road; open daily 9am–7pm; free). There's hardly a native resident in Singapore who hasn't been taken here as a child. This park was opened in 1937 by local millionaire Aw Boon Haw, who built a mansion for his younger brother, Aw Boon Par, on the summit. The Aws made a vast fortune based, in large part, on sales of the famous Tiger Balm.

The amusement park lining the slopes below the villa is lined with garish and often grotesque statuary, telling stories from classical Chinese mythology, literature and folklore. Parents have taken their children here for several generations to expose them to the traditional values – mostly Confucian – behind these stories. The statues originally numbered over a thousand and there were scores of colourful and striking tableaux showing fantastic heroes and villains representing aspects of good and evil, engaged in the primal struggles of life and death.

The Japanese destroyed the mansion during their occupation (1942–5) and it was never replaced, but the park itself was rebuilt. The government then acquired it in 1985 and leased it to a private firm that tried to update the old theme park with high-tech displays and rides. This renovation was a failure. Recently, Haw Par Villa has begun to reverse the tide and return to its roots. The rides are gone and hundreds of statues are coming back, including King Kong-sized gorillas and a Statue of Liberty. No admission is currently charged and local families seem to be finding their way back to this nostalgia-laden attraction. The best sites in the park are the huge tableaux of classic Chinese stories that stand at the summit and the cave called the Ten Courts of Hell, where appropriate punishments for each type of earthly sin are gruesomely and surrealistically inflicted on life-size figures by their tormentors.

Fantastic statuary at Tiger Balm Gardens.

The Feather in Singapore's Cap

Despite its reputation as a concrete island of high-rises, Singapore has over 350 species of birds to delight even the most casual bird-watcher. Early morning, around 7am, is prime spotting time. The Bukit Batok Nature Park is the current hot spot, famed for the endangered Straw-headed Bulbul, first discovered here in 1996. The laced wood-pecker and white-crested laughing thrush provide plenty of auditory entertainment here, too. The Sungei Buloh Nature Park has observation blinds by a mangrove where there's a breeding colony of herons in residence from August to March. The quiet isle of Pulau Ubin, with its mangroves and rain forests, is home to parakeets, owls, kingfishers and hornbills. A good place to start a bird-watching expedition is at the Visitor Centre in the Bukit Timah Nature Preserve, where illustrated field guides are for sale. And from September to March, the white cattle egret takes its winter holiday in Singapore, arriving from as far north as Japan and as far west (or east) as France.

Jurong BirdPark

The largest bird park in Southeast Asia, **Jurong BirdPark** (2 Jurong Hill; open daily 9am–6pm; admission) is located on 20 ha (50 acres) of parkland far west of downtown and is a favourite amusement park of local and visiting families. More than 9,000 birds, representing 600 species, reside here. The hornbill collection is one of the largest in the world. Also the largest in the world is a 30-m (98-ft) high artificial waterfall located at the end of a walk-in aviary, and here 1,500 birds fly freely.

The park can be explored on foot, but there is a monorail (admission) that links the myriad displays. Among the more notable displays are the Southeast Asian Birds Aviary, where a tropical thunderstorm is simulated at noon; the World of Darkness nocturnal house, where snowy owls, night herons and kiwis can be observed in the darkness; and a Parrot Paradise, where the park's most colourful and friendly residents congregate. Other attractions include a penguin pool with 200 of the flightless birds and a lake with an amazing 1,001 pink flamingos. A special highlight is the entertaining 'All Star Birdshow' at 11am and 3pm daily at the open-air Pools Amphitheatre.

It is best to arrive early, before the heat of the day. Visitors can then watch an outdoor show – 'Pelicans, Parrots & Prata' – at the Songbird Terrace, and enjoy a breakfast buffet (9–10.30am) at the same time.

Recently the park, open since 1971, has been emphasising the ecological dimensions of the endangered habitats these exotic birds inhabit in the wild. One new display, The Riverine, offers a river's edge view of over 20 duck species

Making friends with some of the delightfully colourful and companionable species at the Jurong BirdPark.

fishing and nesting in a pristine niche. Their underwater activities, including diving for fish, can be observed through a wide glass portal on a path that runs below the river's surface. The Pelican Cove is another new addition, where visitors can view underwater feeding of pelicans.

Bukit Timah Nature Reserve

If you want to see what outdoor Singapore looked like when Raffles and the first Westerners arrived (and for some 100 million years before that), head for the **Bukit Timah Nature Reserve** (177 Hindhede Drive; open daily 7am–7pm; Tel. 6468 5736; free), located in the northern portion of the island and easily reached by taxi.

This spacious park (164 ha; 400 acres) harbours Singapore's largest surviving virgin lowland rain forest, native vegetation that once covered most of the island. Bukit Timah is a marvellous place to hike, with a series of well-marked trails winding through the hillsides. Bukit Timah is

Like most of the animals in Singapore Zoo, the African lions enjoy spacious and naturalistic enclosures.

the name of the park's summit, the highest point in Singapore at a modest 163 m (535 ft).

Bukit Timah boasts more tree species than are found in the whole of North America. The towering tropical trees provide a canopy for palms, rattans and over 80 species of ferns. Flying lemurs, long-tailed macaques, pangolins (spiny anteaters), mouse deer, giant forest ants, banded woodpeckers and tit babblers are sometimes heard but not often seen.

The Visitor Centre (open daily 8am–8pm) has hiking maps and offers a self-guided exhibit of the park's ecosystem, now managed by the National Parks Board. An uphill hike from the Visitor Centre at the park entrance to the Summit Hut, with its picnic shelter and active lookout on stilts, takes less than 30 minutes each way. The four main trails (and side trails) lead to valleys and large quarries where swimming is permitted. There's also a fine 6-km (3.7-mile) biking trail encircling the parklands.

MacRitchie Reservoir Park

The **MacRitchie Reservoir Park** (open 24 hours daily; free) in the Central Catchment Nature Reseve along Lornie Road is another scenic spot for nature lovers. Boardwalks and walking trails ranging from 3 km to 11 km (2–7 miles), skirt the edge of the reservoir and through the flourishing forest. For the more intrepid, the HSBC **TreeTop Walk** (open Tue–Fri 9am–5pm, Sat–Sun 8.30am–5pm; free) offers good views of the forest canopy from dizzying heights of up to 25 m (82 ft). This 250-m-long (0.16-mile) suspension bridge connects the two highest points in the reservoir park. To get there, visitors must first hike through a 4.5-km (2.8-mile) nature trail. The TreeTop Walk is especially popular on weekends, and with only 30 people allowed on the bridge at one time, the wait to get on can be long. Go on a weekday to avoid the crowds.

Singapore Zoo

The **Singapore Zoo** on 80 Mandai Lake Road (open daily 8.30am–6pm; admission), north of downtown, houses over 3,000 animals and reptiles on its 28 ha (69 acres). One thing that sets the Singapore Zoo above most is its 'open zoo' compounds in which even the most ferocious of animals appear to roam freely. Cleverly concealed features, including moats, cascading streams and vegetation help serve as barriers, although a few glass-fronted enclosures are employed for species that can leap over walls. A lucky few, including some langurs, lemurs and tamarins, are allowed to range freely throughout the zoo.

Getting to know the gentle elephants at the zoo.

Not to be missed are the animal shows, staged at 10.30am, 11.30am, 12.30pm, 2.30pm, 3.30pm and 4pm daily in selected areas (with additional shows on weekends at 1.30pm and 5pm). Most shows are held in the Shaw Foundation Amphitheatre, where sea lions, reptiles or primates take their turns on stage throughout the day. The elephant shows take place as scheduled at the Elephant Ride Area. Animal Friends Shows get under way at the Children's World Animal Land enclosure at 12.30pm and 4pm daily. Note, too, that many animals, from lions and jaguars to monkeys and Komodo dragons, are fed on a regular schedule (times posted daily at the zoo entrance), and this can often lead to some exciting impromptu shows, too. Even the tigers are likely to take a plunge in their pool when the feeding crew arrives.

The zoo also provides a splendid opportunity to have a meal in close proximity to the animals. If you fancy having a 'Jungle Breakfast' (9–10am daily) among orang-utans (the zoo's colony is the largest in the world) and other wildlife, book a place at the Jungle Flavours restaurant in advance. Or get to feed some rare Hamadryas baboons when you hop onto a buggy for a one-hour-long Wild Discoverer Tour (11am, 1.30pm and 3pm daily; admission) into the heart of the forest.

To avoid the crowds, make your zoo visit in the morning (the zoo opens at 8.30am) on a weekday. If you are combining a visit with the Night Safari next door (highly recommended), it is best to take your zoo tour in the afternoon, 3 or 4 hours before the 6pm closing and then walk over to the Night Safari for a cafeteria dinner before the self-guided and tram tours commence at 7.30pm. Both the zoo and the Night Safari are crowded all day every day, as these are two of Singapore's top international attractions.

Night Safari

The world's first night zoo, Singapore's **Night Safari** (open daily 7.30pm–midnight; admission), adjacent to the zoo, has been the island nation's top attraction since its opening in 1994. Covering 40 ha (99 acres), it is a completely different experience. Beginning at dusk (7.30pm), a series of trams, most with witty English-speaking narrators aboard, encircles the eight geographical zones on a 3.2-km (2-mile) paved roadway. Passengers can disembark and take a closer and more leisurely look at the animals in their open enclosures by following one of three walking trails (Fishing Cat, Leopard and Forest Giants).

Set in a dense tropical forest, next to an inlet of the Seletar Reservoir, the Night Safari is a subtly-lit preserve inhabited by over 900 animals representing about 135 species from Asia, Africa and South America. Over 90 percent of the animals in the wild are nocturnal, so this is a chance to see how the animals behave after the heat of the day and the sunlight have vanished.

Perhaps the most entertaining creatures are the fishing cats, slightly larger than domestic felines, who take the plunge to capture trout in a small stream just inches from the pedestrian bridge that passes through their wooded area. The focused, incandescent lighting used to illuminate the fishing cats and other animals makes everything visible to humans, but does not distract the creatures of the night, who are often quite active and seemingly unaware of passers-by. Visitors are separated by natural barriers (moats, vegetation, near-invisible wires) and the lighting system resembles moonlight. Cameras are allowed but flash is prohibited.

The preserve stays open until midnight and many of the park's visitors find the later hours less crowded and more interesting. The twilight world of the Night Safari has given those not inclined to bars, nightclubs and stage shows an after-dark alternative that no other city can beat.

ISLAND EXCURSIONS

Singapore is an island of islands. Some of its 58 nearby islets are now used for petroleum refining and storage, but a few make for excellent day trips, reached by cable car or bridge, in the case of Sentosa, or by ferry or bumboat, in the case of Kusu and Pulau Ubin.

Sentosa

Singapore's fantasy island, **Sentosa**, just south of the main island, is connected by the 710-m (½-mile) Causeway Bridge (open to cars and taxis from 7am until midnight daily). More exciting is the **cable car** ride that drifts 90 m (295 ft) above the harbour into the heart of the island. Cable cars depart continuously from the **HarbourFront Centre** (formerly World Trade Centre) daily starting at 8.30am; last cable cars return from Sentosa at 9pm. The cable car also makes a longer trip from Mount Faber to Sentosa and back daily and offers sky dining (in a glass-bottomed cable car) every Tuesday to Sunday night from 6.30–8.30pm (Tel. 6377-9633 for reservations). The least exciting way of getting to the island is by the **Sentosa Bus** (Sun–Thurs 7am–11pm, Fri–Sat 7am–12.30am) from the HarbourFront Centre Bus Terminal, which conveniently connects to the HarbourFront MRT station.

Views of the world's busiest harbour from the cable car that links downtown Singapore to the island of Sentosa.

*Sentosa Island's
Dragon Court.*

Sentosa originally served as headquarters for the British military in the 18th century, based at Fort Siloso. The island, formerly known as Pulau Blakang Mati, was renamed Sentosa in the 1980s and developed as a resort, with beaches, golf courses, wax museum, aquarium, amusement centres and resort hotels (including Shangri-La's Rasa Sentosa Resort and The Sentosa Resort & Spa).

Western visitors may find the theme island too much like a hygienic Disneyland to be interesting, but to be fair, its recreational opportunities are among Singapore's best, and there are some historical and cultural attractions that are worth touring in their own right. To revitalise some of the island's faded attractions, the authorities are spending a whopping S$8 billion on a 10-year development plan to be completed by 2012.

Free shuttle buses encircle the island, though many of the main attractions are within walking distance of the cable car station at the heart of the northwest portion of the island. Here, the 135-m (360-ft) **Carlsberg Sky Tower** (open 9am–9pm daily; admission) gives a bird's eye view of the Singapore skyline and the neighbouring southern islands. Alternatively, there is a 37-m-high (120-ft) statue of the **Sentosa Merlion** (open 10am–8pm daily; admission), where elevators whisk visitors to its crown and mouth. From the crown, there is a fine view of the island and busy harbour. At night, the Merlion becomes the focus of a towering light show, complete with smoke and laser lights worthy of a psychedelic dragon. Nearby is the dazzling computer-controlled **Musical Fountain** (free) where the Magical Sentosa water, fire and laser lights display takes place each evening at 7.40pm and 8.40pm with a live actor on stage. Other minor attractions include the **Butterfly Park & Insect Kingdom** (open daily 9am–6.30pm; admission), with over 1,500 butterflies and an exhibit of unusual insects, and several interesting gardens and walking trails.

Visitors with children may want to make the rounds of Sentosa's amusement centres located near the Visitor Arrival Centre. Recommended is **Cinemania** (open daily 11am–8pm; admission), where visitors are strapped into computer synchronised seats that simulate every bump and hair-raising moment of roller coaster rides and speed races.

Sentosa's best attraction near the cable car terminal is **Images of Singapore** (open daily 9am–7pm, admission), a fine wax museum housed in the colonial-style former military hospital. This tells Singapore's history and displays its various cultures using life-sized dioramas, artefacts, films and replicas of old street scenes.

Sentosa's other historical display is **Fort Siloso** (open daily 10am–6pm; admission), built in the 1880s by the British to defend Singapore. The creative interactive displays along the underground passages, the cannons and guns, and the video games tell the history of the fort from its construction through to its fall in World War II. Also located here is the **Surrender Chambers**, which brings to life Singapore's formal surrender to the Japanese in 1942 through a gripping mix of real audio-visual footage, artefacts, as well as realistic wax figurines.

Close encounters with the creatures of the deep blue sea at Sentosa Island's Underwater World theme park.

Sentosa is also the location of **Underwater World** (open daily 9am–9pm; admission), a small but excellent aquarium with a submerged acrylic tunnel at its heart. Visitors ride through the main tank on a 'travellator', or moving walkway, while observing the comings and goings of 2,500 sea creatures overhead and on all sides – including turtles, stingrays, sharks, sea cows and monstrous eels, which seem to engulf the 'undersea' viewers. Underwater World also oversees the **Dolphin Lagoon** (open daily 10.30am–6pm; admission) at Palawan Beach, where visitors can enjoy a show or wade in and come face to face with Indo-Pacific Humpback Dolphins, also known as pink dolphins for their unique colouration.

Sentosa levies a small basic admission into the island. Most of the attractions, which are generally open from 9am–7pm daily, levy additional admissions. Various package tickets can be purchased at Sentosa's Visitor Centre (Tel. 1800-736-

8672) upon arrival. All shuttle bus transport on the island is free, and bicycles can also be rented.

Pulau Ubin and Kusu

A popular escape for Singapore residents is provided by nearby **Kusu Island** (Pulau Tembakul) and **St. John's Island** (Pulau Sakijang Bendera). On weekdays, both islands are uncrowded and both offer picnic grounds, changing rooms and swimming beaches. St. John's, the larger of the two, has little else but picnicking and swimming, although the concrete promenades on the shoreline are fine for a stroll and watching the heavy ship traffic in the harbor. Kusu has more to see, including a turtle sanctuary, the Tua Pek Kong Temple at the ferry wharf (a favourite of Taoist worshippers) and the Keramat Kusu Islamic temple at one end of the island, popular with childless couples who come here to pray for offspring.

The island ferry to both islands departs from the Sentosa Ferry Terminal and the ticket includes the admission fee (Mon–Sat 10am and 1.30pm, Sun and public holidays 9am, 11am, 1pm, 3pm and 5pm). The last ferries depart St. John's at 2.45pm (6.15pm on Sun and holidays) and Kusu at 3.15pm (5.50pm Sun and holidays). The schedule changes from year to year (Tel. 6275-0161 for the latest information). Visitors use the ferry to make a survey of both islands.

If time allows a visit to only one of Singapore's little islands, the best choice is **Pulau Ubin**, where some of the last vestiges of old Singapore hang on by their fingertips. Part of the fun is getting there on a bumboat from the Changi Point Ferry Terminal (reached from downtown Singapore via taxi, or MRT to Tanah Merah station, then bus number 2). The bumboat takes about 10 minutes to make the crossing. The first boat leaves Singapore at 6.30am, and the last leaves Pulau Ubin at 10pm. (There's no fixed schedule, they take off as soon as they have 12 passengers.) The village at the wharf on Pulau Ubin hasn't changed in decades, with its cluster of *kelong* (Malay fishing huts), but there are now several businesses renting bicycles by the hour, the ideal way to get around the little island. There's an information kiosk (Tel. 6542-4108) at the village entrance that provides useful maps and offers free guided tours every fourth Saturday of the month at 9.30am and 10am. To participate, visitors simply need to register at the information kiosk 10 minutes before the scheduled times.

The mangrove swamps and coconut palm groves are impressive, as are the duck and prawn farms and granite quarries (Pulau Ubin means 'Granite Island'). The Ma Chor Temple, just above the seashore outside the village, is worth a hike up for its view.

A slow tour of the islet will reveal the remains of rubber plantations, some small Islamic mosques, a half dozen tiny

In the sleepy fishing village of Pulau Ubin you will find the last vestige of old Singapore and its traditional ways.

Island transport is provided by fast and nimble bumboats.

fishing villages where the houses are on stilts, jungle farms and fruit trees laden with papaya, mango, jackfruit and durians. Long-tailed macaques and wild boars also live here, but they are difficult to spot. The island population has dwindled to 200, as the granite quarry business has declined. Some residents still farm and fish, some serve the tourist trade and a few run seafood restaurants. **Noordin Beach** and **Mamam Beach** on the north side of the island attracts swimmers and picnikers, while the quarries that have filled in with water attract adventurous swimmers.

The remote, undeveloped western end of the island is the preserve of an Outward Bound School. The village and jetty are leisurely places to hang out, enjoy a cool drink and relax. For those who wish to spend a night, accommodation is available, on weekends and public holidays, at the **Marina Country Club Ubin Resort** (Tel. 6388-8388; enquiries @marinacountryclub.com.sg). Alternatively, overnight camping is allowed on Noordin Beach and Mamam Beach; no visitor's permit is required.

WHAT TO DO

Shopping and eating are the lifeblood of Singapore. Visitors will find an endless array of places to do both, economically or in high style. There are an increasing number of venues for entertainment and sports, too, as well as an extensive calendar of annual festivals. Nor does any other city offer a better opportunity to introduce children to the pleasure and cultures of Asia.

SHOPPING

If Singapore has a national pastime, it is shopping. The downtown is stuffed with air-conditioned malls, department stores and boutiques, and the ethnic neighbourhoods offer additional street markets and small shops. Most shopping centres and shops are open from 10am to 9pm daily (sometimes later at weekends). Credit cards are widely accepted. Most larger stores and shops do not engage in bartering, but vendors with stalls in markets often do. Many retailers can provide overseas shipping. Insist on written confirmation of the purchase and buy shipping insurance unless covered by your credit card. Shop around to compare prices and quality; test an item before purchasing.

As a free port, Singapore offers a great deal of tax-free shopping. Although a Goods and Services Tax (GST) of 5 percent is levied on all purchases, under the Global Refund Scheme, the GST can be refunded to you if you spend a minimum of S$100 at participating shops. Look for the 'TAX FREE SHOPPING' logo in shops and ask for a Global Refund Cheque to fill in with your purchase. Present all copies of the shopping cheques, the goods, receipts and your passport to the Customs office at Changi Airport Terminal 1 or 2. Then cash your Customs-approved cheques at the nearby

Cash Refund counter (or mail your stamped cheques in later for a refund cash cheque, or a credit to your credit card). You can also claim your GST refund at one of the few Downtown Cash Refund counters straight after shopping (check <www.globalrefund.com> for locations). For more information, call the Global Refund 24-hour hotline (Tel: 6225-6238).

> **English is the common language in this country of many languages.**

The Civic District is dominated by shopping centres, department stores and malls. Some of these are big; others are bigger; and among the biggest is **Suntec City Mall** (3 Temasek Boulevard), the current favourite among Singaporeans. Suntec's shopping towers are much like those in Western cities, although the goods can have an Asian flavour. Its shopping is divided into four zones, with lifestyle products in one

Money-Back Guarantees

Merchants at Changi Airport, providing your last chance to shop in Singapore, now offer two guarantees. The first is on price. If you find you paid more at the airport than at one of the dozen downtown department stores and major shops on their list, they'll give you double the price difference refund if you can show written proof. The second guarantee is simpler. If you bought the wrong gift or changed your mind, they will give you a full refund, no questions asked, if you return the item and receipt within 30 days. You can do this even after leaving Singapore; shipping costs will be refunded as well. For details, fax or write to the manager of the airport shop you bought the item from. For details, write Commercial Division, Civil Aviation Authority of Singapore, Singapore Changi Airport, P.O. Box 1, Singapore 918141.

From huge international malls to traditional shophouses in Little India and Chinatown, Singapore has it all.

and food courts and expensive boutiques in others. French hypermart **Carrefour** offers well-priced groceries, apparel and electronics. The central, circular Fountain of Wealth is billed as the world's largest fountain; its waters flow downward instead of shooting upward, since the traditional Chinese belief is that water represents wealth and the shopkeepers here want the water flowing directly into their shopping centre. Other large malls and shopping arcades in this area include **Millenia Walk** (9 Raffles Boulevard) and **Marina Square Shopping Mall** (6 Raffles Boulevard).

The **Raffles Hotel Shopping Arcade** (328 North Bridge Road) contains art galleries, luxury brand boutiques and

Approved Shops

Shops displaying the CaseTrust (CT) logo are accredited as reliable and honest by the Consumers Association of Singapore.

Traditional souvenir vendor on Clarke Quay.

Raffles Hotel souvenirs at its museum shop. The **Raffles City Shopping Centre** (252 North Bridge Road) nearby is linked to Suntec City Mall by an air-conditioned walkway and shopping mall, appropriately dubbed the **CityLink Mall** (1 Raffles Link).

Orchard Road is another major downtown shopping strip, renowned for its upscale international stores. Among the leading shopping centres are **Wisma Atria** (435 Orchard Road), **Ngee Ann City** (391 Orchard Road), **Paragon** (290 Orchard Road) and **Centrepoint** (176 Orchard Road), home of **Robinsons**, Singapore's oldest department store (since 1858). **Far East Plaza** (14 Scotts Road) has clothing at low prices. **Tangs** (320 Orchard Road) is a delightful emporium with good value buys and a recently revamped fashion section.

The DFS **Galleria** (25 Scotts Road) has a large treasure trove of designer fashion and cosmetics with duty-free savings. At the western end of Orchard Road, down Tanglin Road, **Tanglin Shopping Centre** has the city's largest selection of Persian rugs, antique maps and Asian antiques. At the eastern end of Orchard Road, where it turns into Stamford Road, the **Stamford Court** and **Stamford House** have art and furnishings, while the shop in the **Asian Civilisations Museum** on Armenian Street specialises in gifts and cultural souvenirs.

Other major commercial areas include **Clarke Quay**, with an excellent flea market on Sundays (10am–6pm); **Funan The IT Mall** (109 North Bridge Road), packed with computer stores; electronics at **Sim Lim Square** (1 Rochor Canal); and **Parco Bugis Junction**, a mall that retains its shophouse architecture, with a vendors' night market nearby.

Singapore's ethnic neighbourhoods offer more unusual shopping possibilities. **Chinatown** is headlined by **Yue Hwa Emporium** (70 Eu Tong Sen Street), a department store where the clothing, household goods and crafts are all from China. **People's Park Centre** is filled with Chinese vendors willing to bargain while **People's Park Complex** is a rundown arcade where textiles and clothing can be had for some of the best prices in town, if you're willing to bargain.

Little India is the area to poke around for bangles, gold jewellery, silk saris and Indian spices. The **Little India Arcade** on Serangoon Road has over 50 small shops and the nearby **Tekka Centre** (known locally as KK, or Kandang Kerbau) has a wet market on the first floor and scores of shops above selling saris, batiks, clothing and brassware. **Mustafa Centre** on Syed Alwi Road is a large 24-hour shopping mall popular for its low-priced electronic goods, amongst other bargains like groceries, garments and knick knacks.

The streets of Little India and **Kampong Glam** are a delight to stroll and the small shops offer unusual goods, usually at decent prices (ask for discounts). The **Geylang** and **Katong** districts also offer bargains. This is a Malay area and the Muslim merchants at the **Malay Market** (Joo Chiat and Changi Roads) handle a variety of goods, from batiks and silk scarves to cooking pots and prayer rugs.

Suburban shopping offers many of the same consumer goods available downtown, but often at much better prices. Here, amongst Singapore's towering housing estates, the malls serve the locals who live, eat and shop within an easy walk. Known as the heartlands, these resident malls are becoming Singapore's new towns. Several of the heartlands are served directly by the MRT. The **Century Square mall** is at the Tampines station; **Junction 8** is at the Bishan station; and **IMM** is at the Jurong East station.

The sad fact is that the prices in Singapore on many goods are equal to or higher than in Western countries. Better prices on the same goods are now found throughout Malaysia, Thailand and Indonesia. Nevertheless, if you are not going to these countries to shop, Singapore may be your best chance to pick up Asian items. It never hurts to ask for a discount, either.

Bargain stores do exist in Singapore. The island's version of 'dollar stores', where nothing on the shelves is over the one set price, make for interesting browsing. You'll find items you've never seen before. Keep an eye out for the ABC Bargain Centres and the **Valudollar** shops in the suburban areas. Other discount chains to look out for in the malls include **Sasa** (for cosmetics), **Export Fashion** and **Why Pay More**. The **Cavallino Recycle Shop** (01-45 Tanglin

Complaint Departments

Always efficient, Singapore has several means to rectify retailer malfeasance. You can complain to the Retail Promotion Centre, Block 528, Ang Mo Kio Avenue 10, #02-2387 (Tel. 6458-6377; fax 6458-6393) or you can contact the free online dispute resolution service offered by the E@DR Centre at <www.e-adr.org.sg>. A third choice is to contact the Small Claims Tribunal (#05-00 Apollo Centre, 2 Havelock Road; Tel. 6435-5937; Fax 6435-5994; <www.small claims.gov.sg>), where visitor complaints are heard on short notice and judgments are rendered on the spot.

Shopping Centre, 19 Tanglin Road) has designer fashions and accessories at half price.

Special Shops

Shoppers for Buddhist art and antiques should check out **Lopburi** (01–03/04, Tanglin Place, 91 Tanglin Road; 11am–7pm, Sundays until 4pm). Certificates of authenticity and shipping are provided. There is a big cluster of antiques shops up the road at **Tanglin Shopping Centre** (19 Tanglin Road), including Antiques of the Orient (02–40), Akemi Gallery (02–06),

Bugis Village market offers bargain-price shopping.

Hassan's Carpets (03–01), Naga Arts & Antiques (01–48) and Renee Hoy Galleries (01–44). Nearby, **Antiquity Hands of the Hills** carries Himalayan and Tibetan pieces (Tudor Court, 141 Tanglin Road). **Dempsey Road** is also filled with many tiny, very fine antiques, carpet and Asian collectible shops. **Kwok Gallery** (03–01 Far East Shopping Centre, 545 Orchard Road) has dealt in genuine Chinese dynastic pieces since 1918; and the **Singapore Handicrafts** (72 Eunos Avenue 7, 05-00 Singapore Handicrafts Building, 01-23 The Furniture Mall, and 7500D Beach Road) has stocked a complete range of Chinese carvings, paintings, medicines and rosewood furniture since the 1940s (Mon–Tues and Thurs–Sat 10am–6.30pm, Sun 2–6pm, Wed closed). **Pagoda Street** and **Mosque Street** in Chinatown are also well known for their antiques stores.

Singapore's leading bookstores are **Borders** (Wheelock Place, 501 Orchard Road) and **Kinokuniya** (03–09 Ngee Ann City, 391 Orchard Road), with its huge selection of books covering a wide range of subjects. Both stores have cafés in them. An interesting alternative is the small, independent **Select Books** (03–15 Tanglin Shopping Centre, 19 Tanglin Road), the ideal place to find the Singapore and Southeast Asian books, travel guides and academic studies that the big stores don't carry.

Among custom tailors, **Coloc Tailor** (02–29 Raffles Hotel Arcade, 328 North Bridge Road) can complete a suit in 24 hours. **Gentlemen's Quarters** (03–13 OUB Centre, 1 Raffles Place), in business for three decades, provides overseas shipping. **Mohan's** (02–73 Far East Plaza, 14 Scotts Road) tailors men's and women's fashions, with shirts starting from S\$35 and suits from S\$220.

For something different, find the **Chinese opera** supply shop, **Eng Tiang Huat** (284 River Valley Road; Tel. 6734-3738; open Mon–Sat 10.30am–6pm). Established in 1937, this shop is full of musical instruments, martial arts equipment, opera props and embroidered vests.

One of the best times to shop Singapore's retail shops and malls is during the **Great Singapore Sale**, which runs from the last week in May through June and July. There are good discounts on a wide range of goods during these eight weeks: check <www.greatsingaporesale.com.sg>.

ENTERTAINMENT

In addition to shopping, eating and visiting the cultural attractions of Singapore (including Sentosa and the Night Safari after dark), there is a growing nightlife scene, although it remains a tamer one than those found in some other Asian and Western capitals.

Singapore's **performing arts** programmes bring international East and West entertainers to town. Current attractions are listed in the tourist magazines, such as *Where Singapore* and in the daily newspapers, *The Straits Times*. Check the National Arts Council's website at <www.nac.gov.sg> for updates. Tickets can be purchased through SISTIC outlets (Tel. 6348-5555; <www.sistic.com.sg>) and at Ticketcharge outlets (Tel. 6296-2929; <www.ticketcharge.com.sg>).

Popular Chinese art form: traditional opera.

Visiting Western operas and dance musicals favour the **Kallang Theatre**. The **Fort Canning Centre** hosts outdoor concerts. Singapore has a dozen of its own Chinese opera companies, which often perform on outdoor stages in Chinatown and at annual festivals, particularly at the Festival of the Hungry Ghosts in the early fall.

The relatively new **Esplanade – Theatres on the Bay** gives Singapore a new world-class performing arts centre, an entertainment landmark that many hope will rival Sydney's opera house. Music, theatre, dance and outdoor performances are hosted in this large complex (Tel. 6828-8222; <www.esplanade.com>). This is also where the noted Singapore Symphony Orchestra performs regularly; check <www.sso.org.sg> for programme updates.

Late-night entertainment is spread across hundreds of nightclubs, discos, pubs, lounges, wine bars and karaoke parlours. The dress code at clubs and discos is on the slightly formal side (no sandals, shorts or T-shirts). The top nightclubs and discos are **Zouk**, a trendsetter with wine bar and three clubs (17–21 Jiak Kim Street; Tel. 6738-2988; open Wed–Sat, wine bar open daily); **Bar None** (Marriott Hotel, 320 Orchard Road; Tel. 6831-4657; open daily), where resident local rock band 9Lives packs in the crowds; **Brix** (Grand Hyatt, 10 Scotts Road; Tel. 6416-7107; open daily), a very happening place with beautiful people and special theme nights; **Hard Rock Café** (02–01 HPL House, 50 Cuscaden Road; Tel. 6235-5232; open daily); and **The Liquid Room** (The Gallery Hotel; Tel. 6333-8117; open Wed–Sat; Soundbar open daily) where some of the best international DJs have spun. All have cover charges that usually include one or two drinks; most are open from about 7pm to as late as 3am and till 4am on Friday and Saturday. Other top dancing spots are **China Jump Bar & Grill** (CHIJMES, 30 Victoria Street B1-07; Tel. 6338-9388; open daily) and **New Asia Bar** (Swissôtel The Stamford, 2 Stamford Road; Tel. 6837-3322; open daily).

Singapore's climate is perfect for spending long lazy evenings in the outdoor cafés of Clarke Quay.

The **Mohamed Sultan Road** strip near Robinson Quay, with its restored shophouses, is also a popular stretch, led by clubs and bars such as **Front Page** (No 18 Mohamed Sultan Road) and **Madam Wong's** (No 28 Mohamed Sultan Road). **Robertson Quay** has the stylish **Bar** (01-23 Robertson Walk) and the swanky **Dbl O** (01-24 Robertson Walk).

For those seeking a leisurely drink in the evening, perhaps some music, but not the energetic dance and disco venues of the clubs and discos, Singapore has a large number of stylish bars and lounges, many with outdoor seating. The **Boat Quay** shophouses on the Singapore River now house such establishments as **Harry's Bar** (28 Boat Quay), a favourite haunt of Nick Leeson of the Barings Investment Bank fame; the very homey **Mag's Wine Bar-Bistro** (86 Circular Road); **Fez** (57B Boat Quay), a laidback candle-lit watering hole above Kinara North Indian restaurant; **Molly Malone's Irish Pub** (56 Circular Road); and the very Victorian **Penny Black** (26-27 Boat Quay). Just opposite the river is **Bar Opiume** (Empress Place Waterfront), which attracts a very stylish crowd. And further upriver is **Clarke Quay**, with its restaurants, bars and microbreweries. **Attica** (01-03 Clarke Quay) is the latest hip New York-style dance club.

CHIJMES in the Civic District at 30 Victoria Street offers an Irish Pub, **Father Flanagan's**, which also serves food apart from Guiness and Kilkenny, and **Ocho**, a Spanish-themed tapas bar with a nice al fresco area and good sangria by the jug. Other popular Civic District haunts are **Paulaner Brauhaus** (01-01/02 Time Square@Millenia Walk), the very stylish **Balaclava** (01-01B Suntec City); and the **Long Bar** (Raffles Hotel) where Singapore Slings are must-haves. Around the financial district near Raffles Place MRT are wine at **Bisous Wine Bar** (01-01 Capital Square Three, 25 Church Street) or **Jus de Vie** (Capital Tower, 168 Robinson

Road); and the elegant **Post Bar** in the Fullerton Hotel (1 Fullerton Square). On Club Street, bars with outdoor seats like **Shidong** (7 Club Street) and **Beaujolais** (1 Ann Siang Hill) are great for lounging.

Orchard Road probably has more bars and lounges per block than any other street in Singapore, but the quieter places are on classy **Emerald Hill**, where you'll find a Spanish wine bar, **Que Pasa**; an international cocktail bar, **No. 5**; and just plain beer straight from the tanks of a 1910 Peranakan shophouse, **Ice Cold Beer**. **Sentosa** island offers surfside bars, including **Sunset Bay** (40 Siloso Beach Walk) and **Coastes** (50 Siloso Beach Walk) for intimate cocktails in hammocks.

SPORTS

Singapore has facilities and locations for sports and athletics, but except for indoor pursuits, active visitors should take heed of the high humidity, timing workouts and other exhausting exercises for early morning or after sunset.

Indoors, Singapore offers more than 20 **bowling** alleys of more than 20 lanes. Some alleys are open 24 hours a day; most open about 9am and close an hour or two after midnight. The cost ranges from S$2–4 per line (for information, contact the Singapore Tenpin Bowling Congress, Tel. 6440-7388; <www.singaporebowling.org.sg>). **Bicycling** and **mountain biking** have become increasingly popular, with rentals at Sentosa, East Coast Park, Pasir Ris and on Pulau Ubin.

On the water, **canoeing** and **kayaking** are available at Sentosa, East Coast Park and Changi Point, with single- and double-seaters for rent 9am–6pm daily. **Waterskiing** and **wakeboarding** are available at the Kallang River, where the world championships were once held. **Windsurfing** equipment and small **sailboats** can be rented through the Sea Sports Centre (1212 East Coast Parkway, Tel. 6449-5118), open 9:30am–6.30pm daily.

Scuba diving is offered by charter operators on Sentosa, with trips to Kusu, Sisters Islands and other near points, but the waters around Singapore are not as rewarding to underwater explorers as those in Malaysia, Indonesia and Thailand. The best **swimming** is on nearby islands, such as Sentosa and Kusu, but with such heavy shipping traffic in Singapore waters, most visitors prefer hotel swimming pools.

East Coast Park, located on the shoreline off the East Coast Parkway between Bedok and Marine Parade,

Rollerblading at East Coast Park.

is, like Sentosa Island, given over to fun and especially to sports. Here is a cluster of bowling alleys, bicycle rentals and canoe, and windsurfing outlets for water sports enthusiasts. The Singapore Tennis Centre (1020 East Coast Parkway) is nearby, as is the Laguna National Golf and Country Club (11 Laguna Golf Green).

Golf is extremely popular and several of Singapore's golf courses are world-class, attracting such international tournaments as the Johnnie Walker Classic. There are 11 private golf courses that offer limited access to non-members and four public courses that have no restrictions on visitors. Golfing in Singapore is generally expensive as most members-only clubs charge visitors a premium. Also, weekend rates are often twice as high as weekdays. Private clubs prefer that players hire caddies, or at least a cart and most have a dress code requiring collared polo shirts and proper golf shoes. Many clubs also require a handicap or proficiency-rating certificate. Courses are usually open from dawn to dusk (about 7am–7pm), but a few offer night golf under floodlights, as does the Orchid Country Club (1 Orchid Club Road; Tel. 6750-2112). The private Laguna National Golf and Country Club (11 Laguna Golf Green; Tel. 6542-6888) comes with a premium price, but you get two 18-hole golf courses with stunning, well-maintained greens. The least expensive courses are the public links, but these are all 9 holes or less and only one offers a full-sized par-36 layout (Seletar Base Golf Course, 244 Oxford Street, Seletar Base; Tel. 6481-4745).

Despite the heat and humidity, **hiking** is certainly one of Singapore's most attractive outdoor pursuits. The rain forests of the Bukit Timah Nature Reserve, the wetlands of the Sungei Buloh Wetland Reserve (301 Neo Tiew Crescent; Tel. 6794-1401) and the reservoir greenery of the MacRitchie Nature Trail (located off Thomson Road at the Central Catchment Nature Reserve) are the three most popular trekking areas.

Among the most popular spectator sports in Singapore are the **cricket**, **rugby**, or **field hockey** matches you might chance to see passing by the grassy Padang across from City Hall. Singapore also has its own **soccer** league, with local teams and sometimes international teams competing at Singapore's National Stadium. **Horseracing** under the stars at the Singapore Turf Club (1 Turf Club Avenue, near the Kranji MRT stop; Tel. 6879-1000) is the most popular spectator sport among Singapore's punters. Tourists (over 18 only) can watch the action from the air-conditioned Hibiscus

Room (admission), where the dress code is smart casual. The cheap seats, two levels below and not air-conditioned, have a more casual dress code (shorts, singlets, slippers and sandals without back straps are banned; Bermuda shorts and sleeveless T-shirts are permitted for women only). Swank is the word for this new racecourse, with a capacity of 30,000 betters and served by 500 'totalisator' counters. Races usually commence at 6.30pm Fridays, 2pm Saturdays and 1.30pm Sundays. Call to check the day's racing times. Numbers games (4-D) are also played three times nightly. The horses are imported, mostly from Australia, New Zealand, England, Ireland and the US. This being Singapore, the Turf Club also offers its own food court (over 20 stalls), a public 9-hole golf course (Green Fairways) and a weekly lucky draw on all betting slips. The government's take on bets is 12 percent. Check <www.turfclub.com.sg> for information on race dates.

SINGAPORE FOR CHILDREN

Singapore is a perfect introduction to Asia for children. While there are exotic touches everywhere and the cultures of China, Malaysia and India are much in evidence, Singapore is also highly Westernised. English is widely spoken, familiar fast-food outlets are

Close encounters with the Buddha of Bugis Village.

handy, safety is not a concern and the hygiene is as good (or better) than at home. Best of all, Singapore is a family-oriented society and families are encouraged to do things together. There's a wealth of attractions and entertainment options that are designed for visitors of all ages. Even many of the museums that display history and culture do so with children in mind, employing high-tech films and dioramas to tell their stories. Most attractions offer child discounts.

Sentosa Island *(page 68)* is made for children, with its water park, beach activities, oceanarium and extensive array of amusement parks and rides. The **zoo** *(page 65)* has a special area for younger children and the **Night Safari** *(page 67)* provides something exciting for families to do together after nightfall. The **Jurong BirdPark** *(page 62)* has highly enter-taining shows. Many of the malls and shopping centres have

video arcades. The river cruises and island excursions via bumboats are also as much fun for kids as for adults. A number of other attractions are guaran-teed to keep the kids – locals as well as visitors – entertained.

The **Tiger Balm Gardens** *(page 60)* provide an opportu-nity for foreign kids to experi-ence Chinese culture at one of Asia's oldest amusement parks, one designed with children in mind. **East Coast Park** has bicycle and in-line skating

Sculpture along the Singapore River

rentals. The **Escape Theme Park** (1 Pasir Ris Close; Tel. 6581-9112/3; admission; open Sat–Sun and public and school holidays 10am–8pm) is Singapore's largest theme park, with more than a dozen rides (including go-karts), and acrobatic and juggling performances. The **Singapore Discovery Centre** (510 Upper Jurong Road; Tel. 6792-6188; admission) is filled with interactive displays, virtual reality games and even a shooting gallery. It is currently closed for redevelopment till November 2005.

Temples are full of intriguing details.

The **Singapore Science Centre** (15 Science Centre Road; Tel. 6425-2500; admission), with over 850 exhibits, has an aviation gallery and surround-sound theatre (open Tues–Sun 10am–6pm). Nearby is **Snow City** (Tel. 6337-1511; open Tues–Sun 10.30am–6.30pm, public and school holidays 9am–8pm), where skiing and snowboarding take place indoors year round.

FESTIVALS AND EVENTS

Singapore has a parade of **festivals** that occur in nearly every month of the year. With its multi-ethnic population, these festivals are a microcosm of world religion and culture. Many take place at temples, mosques and religious shrines. Many also take place on dates determined by the lunar calendar or some other non-Western system, so it is vital to check with the Singapore Tourism Board, consult the Touristline (Tel. 1800-736-2000; <www.visitsingapore.com>), or pick up the current festival brochure for exact dates from year to year.

CALENDAR OF EVENTS

January/February *Ponggal:* a celebratory southern Hindu harvest festival, with conch-shell blowing and rice offerings, best seen at Sri Srinivasa Perumal Temple; *Chinese New Year:* fireworks, food, and dragon dances in the streets of Chinatown; *Singapore River Hong Bao:* cultural performances, dances, and fireworks at Marina Promenade and Singapore River, overlapping with Chinese New Year; *Chingay:* Singapore's largest street parade downtown, with floats, stilt-walkers, lion dancers, and roller skaters, marking the end of the two-week Chinese New Year celebrations; *Thaipusam:* the city's most dramatic Hindu festival, a procession of devotees who pierce themselves with skewers and metal structures *(kavadi)*, then undertake the 4-km (2½-mile) pilgrimage from the Sri Srinivasa Perumal Temple to the Sri Thandayuthapani (Chettiar) Temple; *Hari Raya Haji:* this national Islamic holiday marks the sacrifices made by Muslims who undertake the *haj* (pilgrimage to Mecca) with prayers in mosques.

March/April *Qing Ming Festival:* family graves are swept clean, and temples (such as Kong Meng San Phor Kark See on Bright Hill Drive) are jammed with families burning incense; *Birthday of Lao Zi:* followers celebrate the birthday of Lao Zi, founder of Taoism, with a week-long display of performances and rituals at the field next to Sago Lane and Chinatown Complex; *Singapore International Film Festival:* foreign films, seminars and workshops; *Singapore Fashion Festival:* catwalk shows and exhibitions at various malls.

May/June/July *Vesak Day:* Buddhism's holiest day, commemorating the Buddha's entrance into Nirvana, marked by bird releases at various Thai Buddhist temples around the island; *Singapore Airlines International Cup* horse race, the region's biggest, at the Singapore Turf Club in Kranji; *Singapore Dragon Boat Festival:* honouring Qu Yuan, a patri-otic martyr who drowned – the Marina Bay regatta has international races and national championships; the *Great Singapore Sale*: big retail discounts for eight weeks, including all of June and July; *Singapore Arts Festival:* top performers and fringe theatre from East and West; *Singapore International Piano Festival:* featuring international and local nimble-fingered maestros at the Victoria Concert Hall; *Heritage Fest:* one week of multi-cultural events showcasing the country's rich heritage at various venues, such as malls, libraries and museums; *Singapore Food Festival:* an annual gourmet splash that runs throughout July with various special events.

August/September *Festival of the Hungry Ghosts:* the spirits of the dead return in the 7th lunar month, with street banquets, *wayang* (street operas) and shopping for arts and crafts; *National Day:* independence in 1965 is celebrated with massive patriotic parade and fireworks at the Padang; *WOMAD:* a lively outdoor festival of world music and dance at the Fort Canning Park; *Mooncake Festival:* traditional mid-autumn festivities in Chinatown.

October/November/December *Navarathiri Festival:* nine nights devoted to three Hindu goddesses, with Indian music and a procession at Sri Mariamman Temple; *Deepavali:* the Festival of Lights ignites the streets and Hindu temples of Little India; *Thimithi Festival:* devotees fire-walk a 4-m (13-ft) carpet of burning coconut husks at the Sri Mariamman Temple; *Pilgrimage to Kusu Island:* Taoists pray for good fortune and fertility at Tua Pek Kong Temple on tiny 'Turtle Island'; *Singapore Buskers' Festival:* international street performers fly in to entertain with comedy, mime, juggling, acrobatics and magic around the island, including Orchard Road and Changi Airport; *Festival Light-Ups:* seasonal street and shop 'light-ups' begin in Little India (Deepavali Light-Up), spread to Orchard Road (Christmas Light-Up) and Geylang Serai (Hari Raya Light-Up), and conclude in Chinatown (Lunar New Year Light-Up); *ZoukOut Dance Party* sees international DJs spinning from dusk to dawn.

EATING OUT

Singapore is the dining centre of Asia, which makes it one of the premier dining destinations in the world. For food critics, gourmets and hungry travellers inclined to favour Eastern over Western cuisines, Singapore is the best place on Earth to dine. The reasons are many. First, Singapore is situated (geographically, historically and ethnically) on a culinary axis point where several of the world's top cuisines mix and mingle, from the great regional traditions of Chinese and Indian cooking to the more localised and unique cuisines of Malay and the Peranakan (Straits Chinese). Thai, Indonesian, Japanese and Korean foods are also amply represented, as is first-rate fare from the West. Second, dining in Singapore is convenient, with good service the norm and English among the many languages in use everywhere. Third, restaurants are excellent values in Singapore, with hundreds of fine eating choices costing but a few dollars. Fourth, restaurants, even at the street level, are scrupulously clean and hygienic. Lastly, the dining is so varied and the food stalls, cafés and restaurants so numerous (with over 20,000 places to dine), that travellers could not eat their way through Singapore even if they stayed several years.

The chief problem facing a traveller with a few days, or even a few weeks, is where to begin. One way to simplify this delicious dilemma is to make sure to sample each of Singapore's celebrated cuisines. Be sure to try out the various settings for meals, too, from hawker centres and quayside cafés to top hotel restaurants. Ask locals for tips, check out the latest local listings in Singapore's newspapers and magazines, or buy a Singapore dining guide from a local bookstore – but don't deliberate too long. If you see an interesting restaurant, take the plunge. Dining is so competitive in Singapore that one can almost be guaranteed good meals and service, nearly anywhere and at nearly any hour. Singaporeans consider eating an even more important pursuit than shopping, so they pack thousands upon thousands of restaurants nearly around the clock. For dinners, especially on weekends, reservations are a must at establishments that accept them. Otherwise, join the lines; at Singapore cafés, restaurants and food stalls. It is nearly always worth the wait.

Hawker Centres and Food Courts

Hawker centres are Singapore's answer to fast food. While street food and vendors' stalls pose hygienic threats to adventurous diners elsewhere in Asia, in Singapore the outdoor centres encircled by numerous vendors' counters are rigorously inspected for cleanliness. Best of all, meals are extremely inexpensive, with main courses costing just a few Singapore dollars. Frequently, pictures of each dish decorate a food hawker's counter, accompanied by names in English, making ordering a snap. Some of these no-frill eateries are dedicated to a particular cuisine, but most offer a variety of Chinese, Malay and Indian choices, cooked up fresh and on the spot.

Hygiene standards are very high, even at hawker stalls.

Your meal is sometimes brought to you (in which case you may need to tell the vendor your table number); at other times you pick up your order on a tray. Utensils (including knives, forks and spoons) are usually available at the counter. Find a table (which you may have to share) and make the most of the tempting dishes on offer.

Food courts are a fancier version of hawker centres, and often located inside shopping malls. These are air-conditioned, with nicer tables and plates, perhaps, and the price is a little higher, but the same procedures apply. Order from the vendor of choice and wait while your hot meal is quickly prepared. If there aren't custodians circulating, you should do the cleanup yourself.

Some of Singapore's most popular and crowded hawker centres are at **Maxwell Food Centre** near Chinatown, Newton Circus across the Newton MRT, **Lau Pa Sat Market** near Raffles MRT, and in suburban neighbourhoods, while good food courts can be found in nearly all shopping malls.

Chinese Cuisines

The majority of Singaporeans are ethnically Chinese, making the regional cuisines of China the most common offering. Chopsticks are the traditional eating utensil for these meals, although Western utensils can be supplied upon request.

The most common choices at Chinese restaurants and stalls are *dim sum* (small steamed dumplings with a variety of fillings), *char kway teow* (fried rice noodles with clams, Chinese sausage and egg in a sweet black sauce), Peking duck, *popiah* (spring rolls with various fillings), Teochew porridge, wonton mee (minced meat dumpling and roast pork noodles) and *yong tau foo* (stuffed eggplant and bean curd, a Hakka speciality). Undoubtedly the single most popular dish is Hainanese chicken rice (pieces of chicken steamed in stock and served over boiled white rice with a chilli-ginger sauce). Chicken rice is a staple at hawker centres, food courts and most Chinese cafés and restaurants. *Hokkien fried mee* (fried noodles with prawns and pork) is almost a national dish here, as many Singaporean Chinese trace their ancestry to the Fujian (Hokkien) region of China. Teochew dishes originated in the Chaozhou (Chiu Chow) region of southeast China near Guangzhou (Canton), but the food is spicier than the better-known, related Cantonese cuisine. Steamboat is a common Teochew dish in Singapore, a hot pot of steaming broth delivered to the table into which raw vegetables, meats and fish are dipped by the diner.

Singapore's restaurant scene is amply represented by more familiar regional cuisines, such as Cantonese and Szechuan fare. In fact, these are the two most popular Chinese choices. In Singapore, Chinese food is as fine and varied as in China itself; the vast and discerning local population of ethnic Chinese diners insures its quality and authenticity.

You are never very far from a good restaurant in Singapore, whatever your taste in food.

Tea with the Queen

The perfect shopping and sightseeing break in bustling Singapore is a visit to a traditional teahouse. Singapore's best known and largest teahouse is Tea Chapter (9A Neil Road; Tel. 6226-3026; fax 6221-0604; web site <www.tea-chapter.com.sg>; open daily 11am–11pm, located between Chinatown and Tanjong Pagar). On 10 October 1989, Queen Elizabeth II and Prince Philip took their tea here in a private room upstairs overlooking the street. Visitors today can appreciate the pleasures of Chinese tea culture in the same room. The teas run the gamut, from greens to reds, but the service is traditional. First-timers are quickly versed in the art of tea. Water is heated at the table, the tea arrives in tiny packets and scoops, tea clips, fragrance cups, saucers and snacks complete the graceful setting. Guests can linger as long as they choose, savouring the atmosphere of a venerable refuge once the exclusive privilege of British royalty.

Malay Cuisine

Singapore's nearest neighbour, Malaysia, supplies some of the best food in the city. Heavily influenced by Indonesian cooking, Malaysian dishes tend to be hot and spicy, with generous doses of lemongrass, chillies, cloves, tamarind and prawn paste. Coconut milk is also frequently added. For religious reasons, pork is never used.

The chief Malay dish is *satay*, skewers of meat that are spiced and marinated before barbecuing, which sets it apart from the Indonesian version. More difficult to find than strictly Chinese or Indian fare, Malay specialities are worth seeking out at the food stalls. At the Clarke Quay Satay Club, for example, you can purchase mutton, beef or chicken satays served over *ketupat* (rice steamed in coconut leaves), accompanied by *sup kambing* (mutton soup). Among other savoury Malay offerings are *mee rebus* (yellow noodles in a thick spicy gravy), *gado gado* (vegetable salad smothered in a coconut and peanut sauce, served with prawn crackers), *nasi goreng* (fried rice), *soto ayam* (spicy chicken soup with rice cakes) and *rojak* (a sweet and spicy mix of pineapple, cucumber, fried bean curd with prawn paste and peanuts).

Peranakan (Nyonya) Cuisine

Nyonya (which refers to the female member of a Peranakan or Straits-Chinese family of mixed Chinese and Malay heritage) is Singapore's most indigenous cuisine. Chinese and Malay ingredients and recipes have been transformed into some of Singapore's most delicious dishes, with Nyonya restaurants proliferating in the Katong area, in the eastern part of Singapore.

Coconut milk, shrimp paste (*belacan*) and chillies give Nonya dishes a unique flavour. Shrimp paste, chilli and lime are pounded together to form an excellent condiment called *sambal belacan*. Dishes worth trying are *buah keluak* (chicken and black nuts in tamarind sauce), *laksa* (noodles in curry sauce), *nyonya kueh* (rice cakes with coconut and sugar) and *otak-*

Singapore is renowned for its fresh seafood dishes.

otak (minced fish flavoured with lime and coconut, wrapped in banana leaves and charcoal-roasted) – a snack so zesty there are hawker stalls serving almost nothing else.

Indian Cuisine

The Indian food in Singapore is on par with the best dishes prepared in India itself. The ingredients are fresh and the local Indian chefs know what they are doing, especially in preparing curries. In Singapore, diners are treated to the best of Northern and Southern Indian dishes, as well as creations that are uniquely Singaporean.

Northern Indian cuisine is mild and subtle, often employing yoghurt, wheat breads and *ghee* (clarified butter) rather than cooking oils. *Tandoori* (marinated meat or fish cooked in clay ovens) is the signature dish. In Singapore, the

Chicken satay and whole fish on a charcoal grill: typical food of an island that blends many culinary traditions.

local variations on traditional North Indian recipes have led to dishes like *mee goreng* (bean curd, lamb and peas fried with thick noodles in a tomato sauce) and *sup kambing* (a mutton soup accompanied by French bread).

Southern Indian cuisine is spicier and often less pricey. In Singapore, this cuisine is most often served in 'banana-leaf' restaurants, where a banana leaf replaces the plate. Rice is ladled onto the big leaf, followed by mounds of chutneys, *dal* (pureed lentils) and curries. There are no utensils and the meal is eaten by hand, with the rice pinched between one's fingers. For cleanup, use the sink that is a fixture on the wall of any banana-leaf restaurant.

Vegetarians will enjoy Singapore's Southern Indian foods, as many dishes are meatless. Little India has a number of inexpensive vegetarian cafés. Muslim Indian restaurants avoid pork, but they do use other meats, especially in dishes such as *biryani*, which has a basmati-rice base.

Indian cooking is known for its delicious breads, ranging from the unleavened, flat *chapati* to the fluffy *puri*, but in Singapore, one of the most popular Indian breads is known as *roti prata*. This is a large, thin, folded pancake cooked on a hot griddle. When filled with spicy mutton (or chicken) and egg, it becomes *murtabak*, a staple at Indian street stalls and hawker centres. Murtabak is the ideal Indian fast-food and watching the murtabak man at work is far more entertaining than anything seen behind the counters of McDonald's.

Strangely enough, the best known Indian dish in Singapore is not Indian at all, but rather a regional invention, the fish-head curry. The fish head is usually that of a red snapper, boiled up in a spicy, complex curry and served eyeball-up on a banana leaf. During the annual Singapore Food Festival, there's usually a contest for the nation's best fish-head curry.

Cooking Schools

For those who want to learn the secrets of fine Asian cooking and unravel the mysteries of oriental herbs and spices, there are several top culinary schools that can oblige, with introductory courses lasting from a day to several weeks. The at-sunrice academy (Fort Canning Centre, Tel. 6336-3307; fax 6336-9353; <www.at-sunrice.com>) offers hands-on courses with a tour of an Asian spice garden. The Raffles Culinary Academy (02–17, Raffles Hotel Arcade, 1 Beach Road, Tel. 6412-1256; fax 6339-7013; <www.raffleshotel. com>) offers half-day classes Mon to Sat where noted chefs demonstrate the preparation of regional dishes. The Coriander Leaf restaurant (3A Merchant Court, 02-12 River Valley Road, Clarke Quay, Tel. 6732-3354; fax 6732-3374; <www.corianderleaf.com>) has a studio teaching Southeast Asian, Middle Eastern and fusion cuisines.

Other Asian Cuisines

Asian cuisines are well represented by restaurants featuring Korean, Vietnamese, Japanese and particularly Thai dishes. Thai recipes share many ingredients in common with Singapore's other great dishes, including chillies, coconut milk, tamarind, peanuts, noodles and steamed rice, but these are shaped into distinctive creations. At the same time, the overlapping of so many intense Asian foods in tiny Singapore has created what might be called an Asian-fusion cuisine, blurring the distinctions between what is exclusively Cantonese or Malay, Indian or Peranakan in a given dish.

The confusion leads to some marvelous seafood dishes in Singapore, a port where fresh fish is easy to procure. The *al fresco* seafood restaurants along East Coast Parkway do a standing-in-line business nearly every night, but it is difficult to tell if they are Chinese or simply Singapore seafood restaurants. What's on the table is simply the fresh catch of the day, often perfectly prepared in any style you wish, with sauces of your choice. You can have your squid deep fried, your prawns in garlic and your stingray barbecued. Singapore's signature seafood is its chilli crab, followed closely by the pepper crab. These are whole steamed crabs that are infused with a fiery chilli or black pepper sauce – arm yourself with plenty of water at hand.

Another unusual culinary tradition in Singapore is Chinese herbal cuisine. This food is Chinese in origin and medicinal in effect. Principles of *yin* and *yang* are followed in preparing each recipe, and herbs and spices believed to cure specific ailments season the food. Certain items are considered health-giving and curative in themselves, including exotica like fried scorpions, which end up in Singapore's best herbal restaurants – like the Imperial Herbal Restaurant in Metropole Hotel *(see page 139)*.

Ketupat – delicious rice parcels cooked in coconut leaves.

Western Cuisines

French, Italian, European, Mediterranean, Middle Eastern and South American restaurants are scattered across Singapore, where Western food is quite popular, too. Top Western restaurants with foreign chefs are a staple at Singapore's international hotels, of course, but finding an excellent French restaurant with a French chef at the controls in downtown neighbourhoods of Singapore is surprisingly easy. Colonial traditions continue as well, with high tea and tiffin a staple at Raffles, Goodwood Park and a dozen more classy hotels. The American influence in eating is evident in the seemingly ubiquitous fast-food chains, from Pizza Hut to MacDonald's. Not all American invaders are fast-food giants, however. Some of Singapore's best grills, delis, coffee shops and microbreweries are American transplants.

Some of Singapore's restaurants began combining Asian and Western ingredients and techniques even before the culi-

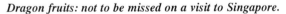

Dragon fruits: not to be missed on a visit to Singapore.

nary revolution of the US West Coast. East-West fusion food, dubbed New Asian cuisine here, places great emphasis on fresh, healthy and simply cooked food and is well worth sampling at such establishments as Doc Cheng's in Raffles Hotel and Club Chinois in Orchard Parade Hotel.

Strange Fruits

One of the delights of exploring Singapore on foot is the market, where all kinds of strange vegetables, spices, fruits and sea creatures are available. Singapore's equatorial location means that tropical fruits head the list of exotic specimens not normally seen in Western supermarkets. The most notorious is the *durian*, known as the king of fruits by Singaporeans. Indeed, this spiny delight fetches royal prices when fresh, but to most outsiders, the smell of the durian is well beyond polite description. Public buildings and the MRT in Singapore still display signs prohibiting the durian's very presence. Singaporeans and many Westerners do like the unusual flavour, however and durian is used in a variety of foods, from desserts to flavoured ice-cream bars.

Among the other fruits commonly found in Singapore's street markets are the *rambutan* (red and hairy in appearance), *mangosteen* (purple outside, white inside), *chiku* (brownish), *starfruit* (aptly named after its shape) and the dramatically red and white *dragon fruit*, whose mild taste is neither smoky nor fiery but tastes of kiwi fruit.

Drinks and Desserts

Singapore serves some superb drinks at its hawker centres, food courts and ethnic restaurants. Ginger tea, a staple of Indian drinks vendors at hawker centres and coffee shops, is a noble contender to the lattes of Starbucks and other coffee invaders. An even more direct contender is *kopi tarik*, the 'pulled coffee' that is poured by the maker from cup to pitcher and back again in a cascading performance. Little India abounds with 'pulled coffee' stalls. The same stunt is pulled with condensed milk and tea to produce *teh tarik*, noted for its delicious foam.

In markets and food courts, try the freshly squeezed juices; they're cheaper and far healthier than canned sodas. Lime and mango can be quite refreshing. Or try a cold glass of soya bean milk or sugar cane juice with a wedge of lemon (easily found at hawker centres). The local beer is Tiger, a refreshing pilsner-style beer. Green teas are still favoured by many Singaporean Chinese, served hot. 'Bubble tea' (also called pearl tea), an import from Taiwan used to be very trendy, but has become a dying fad. You'll still see many bubble tea stands dotting the island, though. At a typical bubble teahouse, the teas are laced with tapioca pearls, shaken until they bubble, then flavoured with fruit syrups, sugar, milk, ice cream – or whatever the flavour of the month happens to be.

Refreshing local desserts, aimed at cooling the day's heat, include *cendol*, shaved ice and green jelly strips drenched with coconut milk and palm sugar, and *ice kacang* (or *ais kacang*), a huge cone of shaved ice festooned with corn, red beans, jelly cubes, evaporated milk and coloured syrups.

'Pulled coffee' ends up with a delicious sweet foam.

HANDY TRAVEL TIPS
An A–Z Summary of Practical Information

Singapore

ACCOMMODATION

There are **hotels** for every budget in Singapore. Major American and international hotel chains are well represented. Most hotels are concentrated in the Civic District (Raffles City, Marina Square areas), on or near Orchard Road and in Chinatown. The Singapore Hotel Association's website, <www.stayinsingapore.com>, offers online hotel reservations. If you arrive without hotel reservations, the Singapore Hotel Association counters at the Changi Airport can arrange bookings. Pensions, hostels and Bed & Breakfast accommodations are few, but there are lots of budget hotels (many with air-conditioning). Travel agents, package travel services and travel web sites offer accommodation deals with substantial savings.

AIRPORT

Singapore Changi Airport (Tel. 6542-1122; web site <www.changi.airport.com.sg>) is frequently rated the best in the world in leading travel publications. Disembarking passengers will discover why, as the march (assisted by travellators) through customs, immigration and baggage claim usually takes just a matter of minutes. There are two large terminals with a third under construction. Clean, modern facilities include full-service banks, currency exchange counters, communication centres with telephone, fax, telegraph, copiers and Internet, post offices, free luggage trolleys, left luggage storage and duty-free shops. There are also hotel and car-rental desks, nurseries, clinics, and restaurant and bar areas serving a wide range of international foods and drinks. Taxis, shuttle vans (the Maxicab) and city buses are available at terminal entrances (a 10-mile/16-km journey to downtown). Taxis cost about S$25 for the ride downtown (including surcharges) while the Maxicab costs S$7 per person. The new MRT link from the airport to City Hall station downtown takes about half-an-hour, and costs only S$1.40.

Arrive two hours early for departing flights. Leaving Singapore, all passengers must pay an airport departure tax (S$21), which is usually incorporated into your air ticket these days. Transit passengers waiting a minimum of five hours may qualify for free city tours (check at the tour counters at Terminals 1 and 2, level 2). A transit hotel is available in both terminals, renting rooms inexpensively in six-hour increments (Tel. 6542-8122; fax 6542-6122; <www.airport-hotel.com.sg>). Showers, saunas and gym facilities are also available for hire for travellers wishing to freshen up during a stopover. The airport and most facilities are open daily 7am–11pm. The flight information hotline (toll-free in Singapore only) is Tel. 1800-542-4422.

B

BUDGETING FOR YOUR TRIP

Singapore has the second-highest standard of living in Asia (behind Japan), so expect many prices to be only slightly below those in North America and Northern Europe. Food and transportation can be bargains. **Meals** at hawker centres and food courts can be as little as S$2. **Subway (MRT)** fares average between S$0.80 and S$1.80. Taxis from the airport are S$20–25; taxi trips around town are considerably less, often as little as S$6; and city buses are still cheaper (S$0.70–1.70). **Hotels** run the gamut, from under S$30 per person for budget choices to over S$500 for top accommodations. Private city **tours** are priced at S$28–100 and up.

Entrance fees to sights are reasonable (S$2–10), but **entertainment** costs (for performances, nightclubs, hotel night spots, bar and lounge drinks) can be as high as in Western capitals. Budget travellers can certainly visit Singapore cheaply, but Thailand, Malaysia, Indonesia and other nearby Southeast Asian destinations offer much lower prices on nearly everything. Singapore offers convenience, cleanliness, efficiency, superb meals and some great attractions, but it is not the bargain basement of Asia.

C

CAR RENTAL

Car rental is seldom necessary in Singapore, since it is compact and served by excellent and inexpensive forms of public transportation, but major car rental companies are in operation all over the island, including at the airport and downtown in the hotel districts. The Singapore government, in a concerted effort to reduce traffic congestion, has made car rental and use, especially in the central business district, an expensive and sometimes complicated affair. Rates for the smallest cars start at around S$150 per day (including insurance, CWD and unlimited mileage).

Rental cars can be taken into Malaysia, but surcharges and gasoline restrictions apply (the tank must be full upon leaving Singapore). A valid driver's license from your country of residence or a valid International Driving License is required, as is a major credit card. Some companies rent cars only to those over 21 and under 60. Despite the fact that oil refineries engulf Singapore's harbour, petrol prices are higher than in some European countries – and up to three times higher than in the US.

Major car rental companies in Singapore include:

Avis: Tel. 6737-1668 in Singapore, Tel. 800/230-4898 in the US; <www.avisworld.com>

Budget: Tel. 6532-4442 in Singapore, Tel. 800/527-0700 in the US; <www.budgetrentacar.com>

Hertz: Tel. 1800-734-4646 in Singapore, Tel. 800/654-3131 in the US; <www.hertz.com>

National: Tel. 6338-8444 in Singapore, Tel. 800/227-7368 in the US; <www.nationalcar.com>

Avis and Hertz are the only car-rental companies at Singapore Changi Airport.

Hotels can often arrange for a car and driver; chauffeur-driven luxury cars can cost S$50 per hour and up.

CLIMATE

Singapore's tropical climate is fairly uniform, as are the hours of sunrise and sunset (6.30–7am / 6.30–7pm), due to its location just 135 km (85 miles) north of the equator. Rainfall is heaviest from November through January. Humidity is routinely very high year-round, (averaging about 80 to 85 percent). Expect daytime temperatures to soar near the average maximum of 31°C (88°F) in the afternoon and night-time lows to dip to near the average minimum of 24°C (75°F) just before sunrise. The lowest temperature ever recorded in Singapore was 19.4°C (68.9°F). Annual rainfall averages 2,337 mm (92 inches), with sudden but brief downpours common. The weather forecast is available by phone, Tel. 6542-7788.

CLOTHING

The island's dress code is casual but neat. Short-sleeved cotton sportswear is acceptable almost everywhere. Even businesspeople seldom wear suits or jackets. Some tourists wear shorts, but Singapore residents seldom do. Mosques require that arms and legs be fully covered (by long-sleeved shirts, long pants and long skirts or sarongs) to enter. Sikh temples require a head covering, as do synagogues for males. Raincoats are hardly necessary, although a light sweater or wrap is sometimes required in the evening. Umbrellas are handy in a downpour. Hats and sunscreen can protect against the ravages of the fierce tropical sun. Comfortable walking shoes, sandals and sunglasses are useful for getting around.

COMPLAINTS

Unsatisfactory retail practices can be reported to the Retail Promotion Centre, Blk 528, Ang Mo Kio Ave 10, #02-2387 (Tel. 6458-6377; fax 6458-6393). Redress from retailers can be secured on short notice, with judgments rendered immediately, at the Small Claims Tribunal, located at #05-00 Apollo Centre, 2 Havelock Road (Tel. 6435-5937; fax 6435-5994; <www.smallclaims.gov.sg>). There is also a free dispute resolution service online at <www.e-adr.org.sg>.

Singapore

CRIME and SAFETY

Singapore has the lowest crime rate in Southeast Asia, but pick-pockets and purse snatchers do operate, usually around neighbourhood markets, even though the penalty for pickpocketing is three years in jail and four strokes of the cane. Crime is also very low in hotels, which have discreet security forces, but use the hotel safety box or room safe for valuables. Report stolen property and other crimes immediately to your hotel and a nearby police station (Tel. 999 or 1800-391-0000).

Remember that Singapore has strict laws covering infractions that might be considered minor elsewhere. Littering can result in a S$1,000 fine for first-time offenders. Smoking is banned in public places, including restaurants and buses and taxis; the fine is S$1,000. The chewing of gum is not banned, but the unauthorised sale of chewing gum is subject to a S$2,000 fine.

Drug offences are dealt with harshly in Singapore. The death penalty is mandatory for those convicted of trafficking, manufacturing, importing, or exporting 15g of heroin, 30g of cocaine, 30g of morphine, 500g of cannabis, 200g of cannabis resin, or 1.2kg of opium. Possession of these quantities is considered *prima facie* evidence of drug trafficking. Those convicted of drug consumption face maximum prison terms of 10 years and a fine of up to S$20,000. Singapore is not the place to bring, buy, or use illegal drugs.

CUSTOMS and ENTRY REQUIREMENTS

Citizens of Australia, New Zealand, South Africa, the United Kingdom, the Republic of Ireland, Canada and the US, as well as of the Commonwealth, Western Europe and South America, need only a valid passport (good for six months) to enter Singapore for a tourist or business visit lasting up to 30 days. Tourists, however, should also carry onward/return tickets to their next destination and sufficient funds for their stay in Singapore. For longer stays, apply to the **Immigration & Checkpoints Authority** (ICA) office (10 Kallang

Road; <www.ica.gov.sg>) or call the hotline (Tel. 6391-6100) upon arrival. Vaccination certificates are required only of passengers who arrive from cholera- or yellow fever-infected areas. An immigration card, supplied before arrival, must be filled out and kept with the passport for surrender upon departure.

There is no limit on the amount of currency or traveller's checks you can bring into Singapore. Customs limitations for personal consumption apply to certain items, including spirits (1 litre), wine or port (1 litre) and beer, stout or ale (1 litre). There are no concessions on cigarettes and other tobacco products (in line with the government's campaign to discourage smoking). Travellers with medicines must bring prescriptions authorising their use. Prohibited items include controlled drugs and psychotropic substances, weapons, ammunition, endangered species and their by-products, firecrackers, seditious and treasonable materials and obscene (pornographic) articles, publications, video tapes and software. A complete list of prohibited, restricted and dutiable goods is available through the Customs Duty Officer, Singapore Changi Airport (Tel. 6542-7058 or 6543-0755).

Lost or stolen passports should be reported to the police; then to ICA (Tel. 6391-6100), where temporary passports are issued; and finally to your embassy.

DRIVING

Motorists drive on the left, overtake on the right and fully yield to pedestrians at designated crossing points. A valid driver's licence or an International Driving Licence is required. Speed limits are 50 km/h (30 mph) in residential areas, 70–90 km/h (40–50 mph) on expressways. Singapore roads are in excellent condition and signposted in English. Speed cameras are installed throughout the island. Bus lanes or lanes with unbroken yellow lines can be used only by buses during rush hours (Mon–Fri 7.30–9.30am, 4.30–7pm; Sat 7.30–9.30am, 11.30am–2pm).

All vehicles entering the Central Business District (CBD) from 7.30am to 7pm from Monday to Friday are required to pay an Electronic Road Pricing (ERP) toll. All vehicles are installed with an In-Vehicle Unit (IU) and a CashCard (stored value card) which automatically deducts the toll from the CashCard each time the vehicle passes through an ERP gantry. Temporary IU devices are available. The toll varies with the time of day and entry point. The ERP is not in operation on Saturday, Sunday and public holidays. There are tolls for using the Causeway and Second Link bridges that connect Singapore and Malaysia.

Driving information is available from the Automobile Association of Singapore (Tel. 6333-8811; <www.aas.com.sg>) and the Land Transport Authority (toll-free 1800-225-5582; <www.lta.gov.sg>). The Automobile Association of Singapore emergency road service operates 24-hours a day (Tel. 6748-9911). The traffic police can be contacted at Tel. 6547-0000.

At public car parks and for on-street parking, a pre-paid parking coupon must be displayed indicating the date and time of arrival. These parking coupons are sold at special kiosks, petrol stations, post offices, 7-Eleven stores and shops throughout the city. Paid parking is also available at most shopping centres and some public buildings. Signs indicate the rates and coupons can be bought from machines to display on the dashboard.

Petrol (gasoline) is sold by the litre (one US gallon equals 3.8 litres; one imperial gallon equals 4.5 litres).

E

ELECTRICITY

Singapore's voltage is 220–240 A.C., 50 Hertz. Most hotels provide a transformer to convert to 110–120 A.C., 60 Hertz. Outlets require plugs with two round large prongs or the three-pronged square type.

Fluid measures

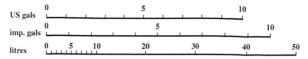

Distance

EMBASSIES, CONSULATES and HIGH COMMISSIONS

Foreign missions and embassies are generally open Monday to Friday, 9am to 5pm, although some work shorter hours.

Australia: High Commission, 25 Napier Road, Tel. 6836-4100.

Canada: High Commission, 14-00 IBM Towers, 80 Anson Road, Tel. 6325-3200.

New Zealand: High Commission, 15-06/10 Ngee Ann City Tower A, 391A Orchard Road, Tel. 6235-9966.

UK: High Commission, 100 Tanglin Road, Tel. 6424-4200.

France: Embassy, 101 Cluny Park Road, Tel. 6880-7800.

Germany: Embassy, 14-00 Far East Shopping Centre, 545 Orchard Road, Tel. 6737-1355.

US: Embassy, 27 Napier Road, Tel. 6476-9100.

EMERGENCIES

If you are in a hotel, call the front desk, operator, or hotel security. General emergency telephone numbers are:

Police	**999**
Ambulance	**995**
Fire	**995**

G

GAY and LESBIAN TRAVELLERS

Homosexual activity is illegal in Singapore. Prison sentences can run from 10 years to life if convicted. This said, there is a discreet homosexual scene, with entertainment venues (mainly in Chinatown) that are spread by word of mouth by people in the community.

GETTING TO SINGAPORE

By air: Singapore is served by about 70 international airlines, representing more than 50 countries. As a major Asian hub, Singapore's Changi Airport is a superb stopover. Relatively inexpensive air tickets to nearby countries can be purchased through hundreds of travel agents in Singapore. Tickets during the high season (June to September and December to January, from Europe and North America; December to January from Australia and New Zealand) are the most expensive.

Singapore Airlines, the national air carrier, is frequently rated the world's best airline. It offers non-stop and one-stop flights to and from many cities, including Vancouver in Canada; Los Angeles, San Francisco and Chicago in the US; Adelaide, Brisbane, Melbourne, Perth and Sydney in Australia; Auckland and Christchurch in New Zealand; London and Manchester in the UK; and Durban and Johannesburg in South Africa (as well as to and from Copenhagen, Frankfurt, Madrid, Paris, Rome and Zurich). Singapore Airlines has offices in all the countries it serves, including the United States (Tel. 800-742-3333), the United Kingdom (Tel. 208-750-2708), Canada (Tel. 800-387-0038), Ireland (Tel. 01-671-0722), Australia (Tel. 02-9350-0100), New Zealand (Tel. 09-379-3209), South Africa (Tel. 011-880-8560) and in Singapore itself (02-38/39 The Paragon, 290 Orchard Road; Tel. 6223-8888; <www.singaporeair.com.sg>). Singapore Airlines provides for early check-in (up to 48 hours in advance) at its Singapore office or over the Internet.

By rail: Visitors can also enter and leave Singapore via bus or rail through Malaysia. Five trains a day, all operated by Keretapi Tanah Melayu Berhad (KTMB) (Tel. 6222-5165 in Singapore; <www.ktmb. com.my>), connect Singapore to Kuala Lumpur and other west coast and central Malaysian cities. A daily International Express Train connects Singapore to Thailand, as does the ultra-upscale Eastern & Orient Express (Tel. 6392-3500 in Singapore, 866-674-3689 in US; <www.orient-express.com>), which takes 41 hours to make the Bangkok–Singapore run. The Singapore Railway Station is on Keppel Road, a 20-minute walk from the Tanjong Pagar MRT station (Tel. 6222-5165).

GUIDES and TOURS

Various private and group tours are offered by Singapore tour companies. These can be booked directly or through hotel tour desks. Use guides licensed and trained by the Singapore Tourism Board (STB). There are city tours, historic tours, tours geared to specific attractions, evening tours and harbour and river tours, as well as specialised tours focusing on food, farming, Chinese opera, *feng shui* (Chinese geomancy) and horseracing. Leading tour operators include the award-winning Holiday Tours (Tel. 6738-2622) and RMG Tours (Tel. 6220-8722). The zany DUCKTours (Tel. 6338-6877; <www.ducktours.com.sg>) take you from land to river as they cover key tourist sights in their amphibious half-boat, half-truck vehicles. The same company also offers HiPPOtours, which are city sightseeing trips on open-top double-decker bus. Visitors can hop on or off at designated stops along the way. Journeys (Tel. 6325-1631; <www.singaporewalks.com>) offer The Original Singapore Walks, which take you to the more unusual places of interest, including 'wet' markets, red-light districts, 'haunted' nooks and graveyards. If it's private taxi tours you prefer, qualified taxi-cum-tourist guides are available: call CityCab (Tel. 6542-5831/ 6542-8297), Comfort (Tel. 6788-8788), or SMRT (Tel. 6555-8888) to arrange.

HEALTH and MEDICAL CARE

Singapore has no free medical care and medical evacuation is very expensive, so be sure that you are covered by your travel insurance. Most hotels have doctors on call around the clock. Singapore's medical facilities are the finest in Asia. The Raffles Medical Clinic (585 North Bridge Road, Tel. 6311-1666) is a 24-hour clinic and the Singapore General Hospital on Outram Road (Tel. 6222-3322 or 1-800-223-0118)) is also always open. For ambulance service, dial 995. Pharmacies are open 9am to 6pm, sometimes later, but it is wise to travel with your own prescriptions and medications. Drink plenty of liquids to avoid heat exhaustion and use sunscreen.

HOLIDAYS

The following state and national holidays are observed throughout Singapore. Banks and government offices are closed on these dates, as are some shops and malls. When a religious holiday falls on a Sunday, the following Monday is usually a national holiday.

New Year's Day	1 January
Chinese New Year	first day of first lunar month; usually in January or February
Hari Raya Haji	Muslim pilgrimage celebration; date changes annually
Good Friday	Friday before Easter Sunday; usually in March or April
Labour Day	1 May

Vesak Day	Buddha's birthday, 8th day of the 4th lunar month; usually in May or June
National Day	9 August
Deepavali	Hindu festival; usually in October/November
Hari Raya Puasa	last day of Ramadan, 9th month of the Islamic calendar; date changes annually
Christmas	25 December

L

LANGUAGE

Singapore has four official languages: English (the language of administration), Chinese (Mandarin), Tamil and Malay. English is widely spoken, making travel by English-speaking tourists a delight. Malay, designated as the National Language, is spoken by only 15 percent of the population, but understood by many Singaporeans. Mandarin Chinese is being pushed by the government as the preferred Chinese language, but Singapore's ethnic Chinese majority speaks one or more of the southern languages as well, including Hokkien, Teochew, Cantonese, Hainanese, Hakka and Foochow. Singapore's ethnic Indians speak Tamil, but many also speak Telugu, Punjabi, Hindi, Bengali and other regional languages. English serves as the island's lingua franca, although the government is attempting to discourage the use of a widespread local form of pidgin known as Singlish, or Singaporean English.

MAPS

Free city maps are available at Changi Airport's arrival hall, most hotels and at travel information centres. The free monthly *The Official Guide & Map* and the *Where Singapore* and *This Week Singapore* magazines also contain maps. Bus/MRT maps are available in subway stations.

Singapore

MEDIA

Of the eight major daily newspapers published in Singapore, four are in English, led by *The Straits Times*, which covers local, regional and international news. *The Edge Singapore* is a business and investment weekly. Local magazines in English include *I–S*, *Where Singapore* and *Eight Days*, all of which cover entertainment, attractions and shopping, while *Wine and Dine* concentrates on dining. International newspapers and magazines are available at bookstores, newsstands, shopping centres and hotel kiosks. Some publications are subject to government-controlled circulation quotas. Magazines such as *Playboy* are banned, as are any publications with articles deemed harmful or offensive to Singapore.

Cable and satellite TV broadcasts, with CNN, BBC, MTV, NHK, ESPN and other common channels, are widely available in hotels. Local TV stations broadcast via the following channels: Channel 5 in English, Channel 8 and Channel U in Chinese; Suria in Malay and Tamil; Central shows arts and documentary programmes; and NewsAsia broadcasts news and current affairs programmes. Three stations from Malaysia are also received in Singapore.

Four of the local radio stations broadcast in English. BBC World News Service is available on short-wave receivers.

MONEY

Currency. The Singapore dollar (abbreviated S$ or SGD) is divided into 100 cents, with coins of 1, 5, 10, 20, 50 cents and S$1. Bills in common circulation are S$1, S$5, S$10, S$20, S$50, S$100, S$500, S$1,000 and S$10,000.

Currency exchange. Money changing services are available at the Changi Airport and at most banks, hotels and shopping complexes. Licensed money changers (usually located in popular shopping malls) mostly give slightly better rates than banks; hotels give the worst rates. The exchange rates at the airport are on par with those at downtown banks.

Credit cards. Major credit cards are widely accepted by Singapore's restaurants, hotels, shops, travel agencies and taxis.

Traveller's cheques. Traveller's cheques are easy to exchange for local currency and are accepted at many stores, restaurants and hotels. Report lost or stolen credit cards immediately to the police (Tel. 1800-353-0000). In Singapore, you can call American Express (Tel. 6880-1111), Diners Club (Tel. 6416-0800), or Mastercard (Tel. 800-110-0113) and Visa (Tel. 800-448-1250) for replacements.

ATMs. Automated teller machines are everywhere (at banks, shopping malls and many hotels). The Cirrus, PLUS and Star system machines work in Singapore just as they do at home.

OPENING TIMES

Museums and tourist attractions have varying hours, but many open about 9.30am and close at 4 or 5pm; some are closed at least one day a week. Banks are usually open Monday to Friday 9.30am to 3pm, Saturdays 9.30am to 12.30pm (but Saturday hours can vary). Government offices operate Monday to Friday 8am to 6pm; some are open on Saturday. Many restaurants are open daily from 11.30am to 10pm, but most hawker centres keep long hours, from dawn to midnight daily. Department stores and shopping centres are generally open daily from 10am to 9pm.

POLICE

To report a crime to the Singapore police, dial 999.

POST OFFICES

Letters and postcards can be dropped off at hotel front desks, which often sell postage. Branches of the Singapore Post are generally open Monday to Friday 8.30am to 5pm and Saturday till 1pm. The

Singapore

Singapore Post branch at 04–15 Takashimaya, Ngee Ann City, 391 Orchard Road (Tel. 6738-6899) is open Monday to Friday 9.30am to 6pm, Saturday 9.30am to 2pm. The Changi Airport Post Office is open daily 8am to 9.30pm at Terminal 2 Departure Hall, and open daily 6am–midnight at Terminal 2 Transit. For post office inquiries and locations, dial 1605. Airborne Express, DHL, FedEx, TNT and UPS provide courier services as well.

PUBLIC TRANSPORTATION

Buses. Singapore has a highly efficient public bus system. Fares are S$0.70 to S$1.40 for non-air-conditioned buses, S$0.80 to S$1.70 for air-conditioned buses. Buses operate daily from 6am to midnight. Ask the driver for the fare to your destination; exact change is required and the money is deposited into a box at the bus entrance which also dispenses tickets.

Alternatively, buy an ez-link fare card (stored-value transportation card), which makes paying easier and is valid on all buses and the MRT subway. With this system, tap or flash your card on the electronic readers located at bus entrances (or turnstiles at MRT stations), which then automatically deducts the maximum fare. When alighting, flash the card again on another reader at the exit, and the unused fare portion is credited back into the card. An ez-link card costs a minimum of S$15 (including a $5 non-refundable deposit), and can be purchased at all TransitLink offices at MRT stations and bus interchanges. A pocket-sized transportation map and information guide, the TransitLink Guide, is a useful buy and can also be purchased at these outlets.

CityBuzz by SBS Transit loops around the city to major places of interest from 10am to 10pm daily. Each trip costs S$1, payable by cash or EZ-Link card, and you can board at the various CityBuzz bus stops; look up the routes on <www.citybuzz.com.sg>.

The Singapore Trolley (Tel. 6339-6833; <www.singaporeexplorer. com.sg/trolley.htm>), a tram bus, drives past major landmarks along

Orchard Road, the Civic District, the Singapore River and Chinatown daily. Unlimited-ride daily tickets (S$9 adult; S$7 children), including a bumboat tour and can be purchased from the trolley driver. Call for more information.

Subway (MRT). Singapore's Mass Rapid Transit (MRT) system is very efficient and simple to use. It operates from 5.30am to midnight daily, with trains arriving every 3 to 8 minutes. Single trip tickets start at S$0.80, in addition to a S$1 refundable deposit. Because this can prove quite cumbersome, it makes more sense to get an ez-link fare card *(see Buses)* even if you're just visiting the country for a day. Rush hours should be avoided. For information, Tel. 1800-336-8900, Monday to Friday. In July 2003, the new North-East MRT line was opened, linking the existing East-West and North-South lines. By 2010, the network will become more extensive with the completion of the round-island Circle Line.

Trishaws. These pedal-driven carts can make for an interesting tour, but be sure to agree on the full fare before boarding. Some tour operators offer city tours by trishaw.

Taxis. Singapore's 18,000 taxis are air-conditioned, comfortable and highly efficient. Most of the drivers are exceptionally friendly and helpful, although a few can be a bit gruff. You can flag down a taxi in the street, but it is best to wait at a taxi stand at hotels, MRT stations, near bus stops and at shopping centres. All taxis are metered; most accept credit cards. Basic fares are S$2.40–3.20 for the first km, S$0.10 for each 250 m (273 yds) thereafter, with extra charges for waiting time. A variety of surcharges are thrown in for midnight to 6am trips (50 percent is added to the meter fare), peak period travel, travel into restricted downtown zones, advanced booking and airport travel. Even with all the surcharges, taxi rides are inexpensive. The three major taxi companies are CityCab (Tel. 6552-2222), Comfort (Tel. 6552-1111) and SMRT (Tel. 6555-8888).

Airport shuttle (MaxiCab). Provided by CityCab, the 6-seat MaxiCab (with luggage storage and wheelchair accessibility) runs daily 6am to midnight every 15 to 30 minutes from Changi Airport to most of the hotels within the city. Inexpensive tickets (S$7 adult; S$5 children) can be booked at airport shuttle counters in the airport terminals. The driver accepts cash or credit cards. Tel. 6553-3880.

 R

RELIGION

Singapore's major religions are Buddhism (42.5 percent), Islam (14.9 percent), Christianity (14.6 percent), Taoism (8.5 percent) and Hinduism (4.0 percent). Other religions, including Judaism, account for 0.6 percent, with 14.8 percent of the population reporting no religious affiliation. Nearly every Christian denomination has a church in Singapore.

 T

TELEPHONE

The country code for Singapore is 65. International calls to Singapore are made by dialing the international access code for the originating country, followed by Singapore's country code and the eight-digit local number. International calls from Singapore are made by dialing the international access code (001, 013 or 019) followed by the country code, area code, and local number.

Most telephones in Singapore operate using phone cards (stored value cards), which can be purchased from all post offices and be used for making local and overseas calls. International calling cards can be used from any phone; simply dial the calling card's access number for Singapore and follow the instructions.

Local calls in Singapore made from from public phones cost S$0.10 for the first three minutes and S$0.10 for every subsequent 3 minutes, up to a maximum of 9 minutes. No area codes are used within Singapore. Dial 100 for local call assistance; dial 104 for overseas call assistance.

Mobile phones: Only users of GSM mobile phones with global roaming service can connect automatically with Singapore's phone networks. If you are planning to be in Singapore for any length of time, it may be more economical to buy a local SIM card from one of the three service providers: Singtel (Tel. 1626 or 6738-0123), M1 (Tel. 1627 or 1800-843-8383) or Starhub (Tel. 1633 or 6825-5000). These cards give you a local mobile number and cost a minimum of S$20. Note: All local mobile numbers begin with '9'.

TICKETS

Tickets to performing arts and athletic events can be booked by phone or in person (and paid for in both cases by credit card) through SISTIC (Tel. 6348-5555; <www.sistic.com.sg>) or Ticketcharge (Tel. 6296-2929; <www.ticketcharge.com.sg>). SISTIC outlets are located at 1 Temasek Avenue (Millenia Walk), 252 North Bridge Road (Raffles City Shopping Centre) and 435 Orchard Road (Wisma Atria). Ticketcharge outlets are located at 176 Orchard Road (Centrepoint) and 163 Tanglin Road (Tanglin Mall).

TIME ZONES

Singapore time is GMT + 8 hours year-round. Thus, in the winter, when it is 6pm in Singapore it is 2am (16 hours earlier) in Los Angeles and Vancouver, 5am (13 hours earlier) in New York and Toronto, 10am (8 hours earlier) in London and Dublin, noon (6 hours earlier) in Johannesburg, 8pm (2 hours later) in Sydney and 10pm (4 hours later) in Auckland. Although the clock is advanced one hour in summer in some countries (such as the US), it stays the same in Singapore. For the time of day in Singapore, Tel. 1711.

TIPPING

Tipping is not the normal practice in Singapore. It is banned at the Changi Airport and discouraged in many hotels and restaurants, where a 10 percent service charge is routinely added to bills on top of GST *(see page 77)* and an additional 1 percent surcharge. Tour guides and drivers appreciate tips (5 to 10 percent) as well. Very small tips (S$1–2) can be paid to taxi drivers, porters and hotel housekeeping staff.

TOILETS

Singapore's public restrooms are reasonably clean and are regularly inspected by health department officials. Most are free, but there's sometimes a nominal charge (S$0.10–S$0.20) for their use.

TOURIST INFORMATION

The Singapore Tourism Board (STB) is a superb organisation, offering mountains of free and helpful literature to visitors. Their website is <www.visitsingapore.com>.

STB offices abroad include the following:

Australia: Singapore Tourism Board, Level 11, AWA Building, 47 York Street, Sydney NSW 2000; Tel. (61-2) 9290-2888 or 9290-2882; fax (61-2) 9290-2555. Singapore Tourism Board, Representative Office, c/o Power Travel Consulting, 1 Spencer Street, Hawthorn, VIC 3122; Tel. (61-3) 9815-1986; fax (61-3) 9815-2986. Singapore Tourism Board, Representative Office, c/o Devahasdin PR, 15 Lawrence Avenue, West Perth WA 6005; Tel. (61-8) 9226-5666; fax (61-8) 9226-2444.

New Zealand: Singapore Tourism Board, Representative Office, c/o Vivaldi World Limited, Suite 10K, 18 Ronwood Avenue, Manukau City, Aukland 1702; Tel. (64-9) 262-3933; fax (64-9) 262-3927.

UK: Singapore Tourism Board, 1st floor, Carrington House, 126-130 Regent Street, London W1B 5JX; Tel. (44-207) 437-0033, (08080) 656565; fax (44-207) 734-2191.

US: Singapore Tourism Board, 4929 Wilshire Boulevard, Suite 510, Beverly Hills, CA 90010; Tel. (323) 677-0808; fax (323) 677-0801. Singapore Tourism Board, 1156 Avenue of the Americas, Suite 702, New York, NY 10036; Tel. (212) 302-4861; fax (212) 302-4801.

In **Singapore**, the efficient Singapore Tourism Board runs a 24-hour tourist information hotline (toll-free in Singapore): Tel. 1800-736-2000. In addition, visitor centres are located at the following locations:

Singapore Changi Airport: Terminals 1 and 2, Arrival Halls; open daily 6am–2am

Orchard Road: open daily 8am–10.30pm, Tel. 1800-736-2000

Suntec City Mall: 01-35, The Galleria@Suntec City Mall, 3 Temasek Boulevard; open daily 10am–6pm; Tel. 1800-332-5066

Liang Court: Level 1, 177 River Valley Road; open daily 10am–10pm; Tel. 6336-7184

Inncrowd Backpackers' Hostel: Little India, 73 Dunlop Street; open daily 10am–10pm; Tel. 6296-4280

WATER

Due to its limited natural resources, Singapore has long depended on neighbouring Malaysia for most of its water supply. In an effort to be more self-sufficient, since February 2003, Singaporeans have slowly been getting used to Newater, a catchword for reclaimed water which has been put through a rigorous purification process. Only a trickle of Newater is mixed into reservoir water currently – just 1 percent of the 300 million gallons consumed daily. By 2011 the proportion is targeted to increase to about 2.5 percent. Despite this, tap water is perfectly safe to drink in Singapore. Bottled water (local and international brands) is widely available for purchase.

WEBSITES

The Internet provides many sites for information about Singapore.

<www.changi.airport.com.sg> Changi Airport.

<www.stayinsingapore.com> Hotel site for on-line bookings.

<www.nhb.gov.sg> Museums in Singapore.

<www.singaporeair.com> Singapore Airlines.

Singapore

<www.visitsingapore.com> Singapore Tourism Board (STB).
<www.asia1.com.sg> Media site with useful links.
<www.esplanade.com> Esplanade–Theatres on the Bay
programme details.
<www.gov.sg> Official Singapore Government site.

WEIGHTS and MEASURES

Length

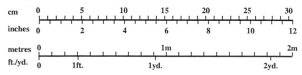

Weight

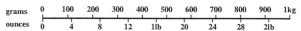

Temperature

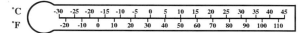

YOUTH HOSTELS

Singapore has no youth hostels, but some inexpensive 'backpacker'
inns offer dormitories and small rooms with shared baths. The
Singapore Tourism Board's free *Accommodation Guide* lists dozens
of economical lodgings, with descriptions and contact information.
Hangout@Mt.Emily (*10A Upper Wilkie Road, Singapore 228119;
Tel. 6438-5588, fax 6339-6008; <www.hangouthotels.com>*) is a
new and funky budget-class hotel conveniently located near the
Civic District.

Recommended Hotels

Singapore has several of the world's top-rated luxury hotels, a number of new boutique hotels, and some of the cleanest budget rooms in Asia.

Posted hotel prices tend to be fairly expensive, but hefty discounts are common. Occupancy is at its highest during the high season (August and December to the end of Chinese New Year) and reservations are recommended. You can book a room yourself on the Singapore Hotel Association's web site <www.stayinsingapore.com>, which includes full descriptions, rates, and specials for nearly every hotel and inn in Singapore.

All accommodations take major credit cards, except where noted. Meals are normally not included, although some hotels and resorts have package specials that include buffet breakfasts.

Each entry is marked with a symbol indicating the approximate room rate charged, per night, for a double room with bath. Prices do not include the 10 percent service charge, 5 percent goods and services tax, and 1 percent government entertainment tax, except where noted.

$	up to S$80
$$	S$80–150
$$$	S$150–250
$$$$	S$250–350
$$$$$	S$350 and more

Berjaya Hotel $$$ *83 Duxton Road, Singapore 089540; Tel. 6227-7678; fax 6227-1232. Website <www.berjayaresorts.com>.* One of Chinatown's most elegant boutique hotels, the Berjaya (formerly the Duxton) decorates its rooms with colonial and Straits Chinese furnishings. Near the business district. 48 rooms.

Conrad Centennial Singapore $$$$ *2 Temasek Boulevard, Singapore 038982; Tel. 6334-8888; fax 6333-9166. Website <www.conradhotels.com>.* Geared to upscale business travellers, this luxury hotel is located closest to Suntec City. It provides large rooms and top services. Disabled access. 509 rooms.

Fort Canning Lodge YWCA $$ *6 Fort Canning Road, Singapore 179494; Tel. 6338-4222; fax 6337-4222. Website <www.ywca. org.sg>.* Recently renovated and in a quiet neighbourhood, the YWCA has dorms and rooms, some with private baths, for single women, couples and families. 212 rooms.

Four Seasons $$$$–$$$$$ *190 Orchard Road, Singapore 248646; Tel. 6734-1110; fax 6733-0682. Website <www.fourseasons.com/ singapore>.* Built to compete with Asia's most upscale hotels, the elegant Four Seasons has a prime location and a vast fitness and recreation centre. Disabled access. 254 rooms.

The Fullerton $$$$–$$$$$ *1 Fullerton Square, Singapore 049178; Tel. 6733-8388; fax 6735-8388. Website <www.fullertonhotel.com>.* Created within a 1928 colonial landmark fronting Marina Bay, the Fullerton is aiming to become Asia's top upscale hotel, with grand facilities and services to match. Disabled access. 400 rooms.

The Gallery Hotel $$–$$$$ *76 Robertson Quay, Singapore 238254; Tel. 6849-8686; fax 6836-6666. Website <www.galleryhotel. com.sg>* Overlooking the Singapore River, Singapore's award-winning boutique hotel brings high-tech style to its compact rooms. Free internet access in every room. Disabled access. 222 rooms.

Goodwood Park $$$$ *22 Scotts Road, Singapore 228221; Tel. 6737-7411; fax 6732-8558. Website <www.goodwoodparkhotel. com.sg>.* A National Landmark, dating from 1900, this grand hotel in expansive gardens off Orchard Road is renowned for its service, dining and romantic interiors. 235 rooms.

Grand Copthorne Waterfront $$$ *392 Havelock Road, Singapore 169663; Tel. 6733-0880; fax 6737-8880. Website <www.millennium hotels.com>.* Luxury hotel located right on the Singapore River, the Grand Copthorne has a marvellous riverside ambience and al fresco dining. Disabled access. 538 rooms.

Grand Hyatt $$$$ *10 Scotts Road, Singapore 228211; Tel. 6738-1234; fax 6732-1696. Website <www.singapore.hyatt.com>.* A stone's throw from Orchard Road, this top luxury hotel for over three decades has turned half its rooms into large business suites for business travellers. Disabled access. 693 rooms.

Grand Plaza Parkroyal $$–$$$ *10 Coleman Street, Singapore 179809; Tel. 6336-3456; fax 6339-9311. Website <www.parkroyal hotels.com>.* Located in the historic Civic District, this luxury hotel has an excellent spa. Disabled access. 326 rooms.

Hilton International $$$$ *581 Orchard Road, Singapore 238883; Tel. 6737-2233; fax 6732-2917. Website <www.hilton.com>.* Since 1970, the Hilton has been a favourite of business travellers for its central location, rooftop pool and good dining. Disabled access. 423 rooms.

Holiday Inn Park View Singapore $$$ *11 Cavenagh Road, Singapore 229616; Tel. 6733-8333; fax 6734-4593. Website <www.singapore.holiday-inn.com>.* North of Orchard Road near Istana, this Holiday Inn has clean, modern rooms, an efficient staff and a top-rated Indian restaurant. Disabled access. 311 rooms.

Hotel New Otani Singapore $$$ *177A River Valley Road, Singapore 179031; Tel. 6338-3333; fax 6339-2854. Website <www.newotanisingapore.com>.* Perched on Clarke Quay, the New Otani has modern rooms with balconies and offers organized walking tours and free Singapore River cruises. 408 rooms.

Hotel Phoenix $$ *277 Orchard Road, Singapore 238858; Tel. 6737-8666; fax 6732-2024. Website <www.hotelphoenixsingapore.*

com>. Excellent value for its fantastic location on Orchard Road. Next door to the Somerset MRT station. All rooms have personal computers with e-mail and internet access. Coffee house, lobby lounge and pastry shop. 392 rooms.

Inter-Continental $$$$ *80 Middle Road, Singapore 188966; Tel. 6338-7600; fax 6338-7366. Website <www.singapore.interconti. com>*. Built over Bugis Street, this award-winning luxury tower offers shophouse theme rooms with Peranakan artefacts. Disabled access. 406 rooms.

Marriott $$$$ *320 Orchard Road, Singapore 238865; Tel. 6735-5800; fax 6735-9800. Website <www.marriotthotels.com>*. Located right at the corner of Orchard and Scotts Roads, this Marriott has spacious rooms and a contemporary Chinese décor inside and out. Disabled access. 373 rooms.

Meritus Mandarin $$$$ *333 Orchard Road, Singapore 238867; Tel. 6737-4411; fax 6732-2361. Website <www.mandarin-singapore. com>*. This towering luxury hotel, recently renovated, is topped by Singapore's highest revolving restaurant. 1,200 rooms.

Metropole $$ *41 Seah Street, Singapore 188396; Tel. 6336-3611; fax 6339-3610. Website <www.metrohotel.com>*. A good mid-range hotel, next to the Raffles Hotel, the no-frills Metropole offers clean, modern rooms and free continental breakfast. 54 rooms.

Pan-Pacific $$$$ *7 Raffles Boulevard, Marina Square, Singapore 039595; Tel. 6336-8111; fax 6339-1861. Website <www.singapore. panpac.com>*. Marina Square's least expensive, most spacious modern hotel is quite luxurious, recently remodelled, with spectac-ular views of the harbour. 784 rooms.

Perak Lodge $ *12 Perak Road; Tel. 6229-7733; fax 6392-0919. Website <www.peraklodge.net>*. Occupying a restored shophouse in Little India, this budget-class hotel has ensuite rooms with air-conditioning and TV. There is also a lovely restaurant, served by friendly staff. 34 rooms.

Raffles Hotel $$$$$ *1 Beach Road, Singapore 189673; Tel. 6337-1886; fax 6339-7650. Website <www.raffleshotel.com>.* Since 1887, Raffles has been one of the legendary hotels of Asia. Recently restored to an all-suites hotel, this National Monument is thoroughly plush and historic, worthy of Singapore's highest room rates. Disabled access. 103 rooms.

The Regent $$$$ *1 Cuscaden Road, Singapore 249715; Tel. 6733-8888; fax 6732-8838. Website <www.regenthotels.com>.* Located a few blocks south of Orchard Road in the Tanglin shopping area, the Regent is a majestic modern hotel with fairly large rooms, an airy atrium and a relaxing atmosphere. Disabled access. 441 rooms.

The Ritz-Carlton, Millenia $$$$ *7 Raffles Avenue, Singapore 039799; Tel. 6337-8888; fax 6338-0001. Website <www.ritzcarlton.com>.* A luxury hotel with a view and larger than average rooms, the Ritz-Carlton's 32-storey tower at Marina Bay overlooks the harbour, the city and Millenia Walk shopping mall. Disabled access. 610 rooms.

The Scarlet $$–$$$ *33 Erskine Road, Singapore 069333; Tel. 6511-3333; fax 6511-3303. Website <www.thescarlethotel.com>.* Located near Chinatown, this newly-opened boutique hotel is luxurious and dramatic, with characterful ensuite rooms. 84 rooms.

Shangri-La $$$$ *22 Orange Grove Road, Singapore 258350; Tel. 6737-3644; fax 6737-3257. Website <www.shangri-la.com>.* For more than 30 years, the Shangri-La's flagship hotel in Singapore has won numerous international awards, deservedly so given its high level of service, spacious rooms, fine dining and commanding location on a large garden estate near Orchard Road. Disabled access. 760 rooms.

Shangri-La's Rasa Sentosa Resort $$$–$$$$ *101 Siloso Road, Sentosa, Singapore 098970; Tel. 6275-0100; fax 6275-0355. Website*

Singapore

<www.shangri-la.com>. Located on Sentosa Island, Singapore's top resort hotel offers a free downtown shuttle bus service, a fine buffet breakfast, free watersports equipment and more. Disabled access. 459 rooms.

SHA **Villa** $$ *64 Lloyd Road, Singapore 239113; Tel. 6299-6007; fax 6299-9827. E-mail <hoteleng@online.com.sg>*. Several blocks south of Orchard Road, this small boutique hotel occupies a three-storey colonial mansion with Peranakan décor. 43 rooms.

Sheraton Towers $$$$ *39 Scotts Road, Singapore 228230; Tel. 6737-6888; fax 6737-1072. Website <www.sheraton.com/towers singapore>*. With butlers for all rooms and amenities galore, this is one of the most luxurious Sheratons in the world. 413 rooms.

Swissôtel The Stamford $$$$ *2 Stamford Road, Singapore 178882; Tel. 6338-8585; fax 6338-2862. Website <www.singapore-stamford.swissotel.com>*. Until recently the world's tallest hotel, this is still Singapore's largest. The adjacent Raffles The Plaza adds 769 equally fine rooms to the complex. Major renovations recently completed. Disabled access. 1,200 rooms.

Traders Hotel Singapore $$$ *1A Cuscaden Road, Singapore 249716; Tel. 6738-2222; fax 6831-4314. Website <www.shangri-la.com>*. Sister hotel to the upscale Shangri-La, Traders is both comfortable and practical, with excellent services and rooms, self-service laundry facilities, a refrigerator, large swimming pool and a skywalk to a shopping mall, grocery and food court on Tanglin, all at affordable rates. Disabled access. 547 rooms.

YMCA International House $$ *1 Orchard Road, Singapore 238824; Tel. 6235-2498; fax 6235 1416. Website <www.ymca.org.sg>*. A popular air-conditioned budget hotel, this Y on Orchard Road has single, twin and family rooms, and dorms. Restaurant and McDonald's on premises. Requires advanced booking. 111 rooms.

Recommended Restaurants

Singapore, with over 20,000 restaurants, cafés and food courts, has dining options to fit every taste and budget. The major cuisines are Chinese, Malay, Peranakan (a local fusion of Chinese and Malay) and Indian (both southern and northern), with healthy infusions of Indonesian, Thai and other Southeast Asian foods. There are also many fine American, South American and European restaurants. Critics often hail the Asian dining in Singapore as the world's best, owing to its fresh seafood and other ingredients, its obsession with culinary matters and its position at the crossroads of Chinese, Malay and Indian dining traditions. In general, wherever one eats, from hawker centres to top international hotel restaurants, the food and service are likely to be first-rate.

Each entry is marked with a symbol indicating the price range, per person, for a three-course dinner or equivalent (drinks, gratuities and taxes are not included). Lunch in the same restaurant will be less expensive than dinner.

$	up to S$10
$$	S$10–20
$$$	S$20–40
$$$$	S$40 and more

Ah Hoi's Kitchen $$–$$$ *4th floor, Trader's Hotel, 1A Cuscaden Road, Civic District; Tel. 6831-4373.* Open daily for lunch and dinner. Ah Hoi's has many superb local favourites, including fried black pepper *kway teow* (rice noodles) with seafood (Teochew style prawns, fish and squid) and an unparalleled selection of stir-fried crabs in the shell, from chilii crab to pepper crab and beyond. Casual dining at its best, with the Ah Hoi 'pancake' recommended for dessert. Major credit cards.

Singapore

Blu $$$$ *24/F Shangri-La Hotel, 22 Orange Grove Road; Tel. 6213-4598.* Open Monday to Saturday for dinner, closed Sunday. With a stunning view above the west end of Orchard Road and a swank bar, Blu has become a trendy, elegant night spot to enjoy the new California fusion cuisine, excellent live jazz, international wines and French champagne by the glass. Major credit cards.

Boon Tong Kee $–$$ *399 Balestier Road; Tel. 6256-0138.* Open daily for lunch and dinner. This no-frills sidewalk café serves Hainanese chicken rice dishes that locals drive miles to consume. No credit cards.

Chef Chan's Restaurant $$–$$$ *01-02 Odeon Towers, 331 North Bridge Road Tel: 6250 3363.* Unconventional black walls, chefs clad in black jackets, and huge Chinese lanterns imported from Guangzhou, and the chef's personal collection of Chinese antiques, is the setting for the innovative Cantonese cuisine served here. Signature dishes are crispy roast chicken, black-pepper beef tenderloin, and braised shark's fin with crab roe.

Colours by the Bay $$–$$$ *01-13A/G, Esplanade Mall, The Esplanade – Theatres on the Bay, 8 Raffles Avenue; Tel. 6835-7988.* Open daily lunch and dinner. Theater-goers to The Esplanade – Theatres on the Bay are spoilt for choice here, where seven restaurants are housed in one venue. You could be dining on Italian, while your dining companions select from Chinese, Japanese, Thai, noodles, Italian or even garlic-inspired dishes from the aptly named Garlic Restaurant. Major credit cards.

Crossroads Café $$ *Marriott Hotel, 320 Orchard Road; Tel. 6831 4605.* Perch yourself at this sidewalk café and watch all of Orchard Road pass by while you sample its varied and delicious mix of Asian and Western dishes.

Doc Cheng's $$$–$$$$ *02–19 Raffles Hotel, 1 Beach Road; Tel. 6337-1886.* Open Monday to Friday for lunch, daily for dinner. Doc

Cheng's combines all the major Asian cuisines with the latest trends from the West to produce some real surprises. Major credit cards.

Esmirada $$$–$$$$ *01-00 Orchard Hotel, 442 Orchard Road; Tel. 6735-3476.* Open daily for lunch and dinner. Lively restaurant and wine bar that serves authentic hearty Mediterranean fare. Special vegetarian menus available for non-meat eaters. Major credit cards.

The Forbidden City $$$–$$$$ *3A Merchant's Court, River Valley Road, #01-02 Clarke Quay; Tel. 6557-6266.* Open daily for lunch and dinner. This lush, stylish eatery, housed in a magnificent two-storey pre-war building, serves modern Chinese cuisine. Proceed to the bar on the first floor for post-dinner drinks. Major credit cards.

Hajjah Maimunah $ *11 Jalan Pisang; Tel. 6291-3132.* Open Mon–Sat for lunch and dinner. No-frills eatery that serves some of the best Malay food in town. Just point to the dishes behind the glass counter and indicate how many of you are eating. The tender beef *rendang* curry just melts in your mouth. No credit cards.

House of Peranakan Cuisine $$–$$$ *Meritus Negara Hotel, 10 Claymore Road, Tel. 6733-4411.* Open daily lunch and dinner. This Straits Chinese (Peranakan) cuisine restaurant serves perennial favourites like *sambal* (chilli) long beans and *otak otak* (barbecued spicy fish paste). Major credit cards.

Imperial Herbal $$$–$$$$ *Metropole Hotel, 41 Seah Street; Tel. 6337-0491.* Open daily for lunch and dinner. This traditional Chinese restaurant has devised tasty medicinal dishes to treat whatever ails you, from the common cold to impotence, by restoring your internal yin and yang balance. Herbal doctors are on hand to prescribe some devilishly good tonics, herbs and entrées, including a divine Eight Treasures Chicken. Major credit cards.

Komala Vilas $–$$ *76-78 Serangoon Road, Little India; Tel. 6293-6980.* Open daily. Singapore's classic southern Indian vegetarian restaurant (six decades old) provides an unforgettable dining experience with its spicy rice and lentil curries served on a banana leaf, its chutneys and its *dosai* (vegetable-stuffed crêpes). Eat with your hands; wash up at sinks on the wall. No credit cards.

Lei Garden $$$$ *#01–24 CHIJMES, 30 Victoria Street, Civic District; Tel. 6339-3822.* Open daily for lunch and dinner. One of Singapore's best Cantonese restaurants, in an exquisite formal setting, Lei Garden is renowned for its *dim sum* lunches and fresh seafood dishes (shark, abalone, lobster). Major credit cards.

The Line $$$–$$$$ *Shangri-La Hotel, 22 Orange Grove Road; Tel. 6737-3644.* Open daily. This all-day dining buffet restaurant is one of the most stylish buffet restaurants in town. The 16 culinary stations turn out freshly prepared international fare, from wood-fired pizzas to *sushi* and *dim sum*. Major credit cards.

Little India Arcade $ *48 Serangoon Road, Little India; no phone.* Open daily. At the back of this shopping arcade is Hastings Food Court, a small treasure trove for Indian curries, Malay dishes and drawn teas. Pick a table and order from one of the counters; the dishes are served on banana leaves. No credit cards.

Muthu's Curry $–$$ *138 Race Course Road, Little India; Tel. 6392-1722.* Open daily. This 35-year-old restaurant serves a potent fish head curry (its award-winning speciality), and other delicious dishes – all served on banana leaves instead of plates.

My Humble House $$$–$$$$ *#02-27/29, Esplanade Mall, 8 Raffles Avenue; Tel. 6423-1881.* Open daily lunch and dinner. Despite its name, this grand restaurant is anything but modest. Expect to be wowed by elaborately luxurious interiors and delicate Chinese cuisine that comes with poetic names. Major credit cards.

Original Sin $$–$$$ *Jalan Merah Saga, Block 43, #01–62 Chip Bee Gardens, Holland Village District; Tel. 6475-5605.* Open

Tuesday to Sunday for lunch, daily for dinner. This vegetarian restaurant specializes in Italian and Mediterranean fare, with knock-out, mock-meat cannelloni and pizzas, as well as superb risotto, pasta and salads, in a European setting. Major credit cards.

Red House Seafood $$–$$$ *Block 1204, #01–05 East Coast Seafood Centre; Tel. 6442-3112.* Open daily for dinner. The breezy seashore along the East Coast Parkway has a dozen good seafood restaurants at the East Coast Seafood Centre; Red House is one of the best and most crowded (no reservations), offering informal outdoor seafood dining at its best and noisiest, with superb chilli crab and drunken prawns leading the pack. Major credit cards.

Saint Pierre $$$$ *#01–01 Central Mall, 3 Magazine Road; Tel. 6438-0887.* Open Monday to Friday for lunch and dinner, Saturday for dinner only, closed Sunday. One of the top spots in Singapore for high-end French dining given a Japanese twist. Stylish setting is the perfect foil for innovative *foie gras* dishes. Top favourites include black cod in miso sauce and desserts like Grandma Stroobant's flourless chocolate cake. Major credit cards.

Sanur $$–$$$ *#04–17/18 Centrepoint, 179 Orchard Road; Tel. 6734-2192.* Open daily for lunch and dinner. The excellent Indonesian and Malay dishes include *tahu telur*, a towering beancurd and soy sauce omelet. This is a good place for *gado gado* and *rojak*, too. Further branches are located in Ngee Ann City (391 Orchard Road), Parco Bugis Junction (200 Victoria Street) and the basement of Suntec City (5 Temasek Boulevard). Major credit cards.

Satay Club $–$$ *Read Street, Clarke Quay; no phone.* Open daily for dinner. A score of street vendors barbecue skewers of mutton, beef, or chicken, served over rice on coconut leaves nightly on the bank of the Singapore River. The mutton soup (*sup kambing*) and fried noodles (*mamak mee goreng*) are also tasty. No credit cards.

Singapore

Sharkey's $$$–$$$$ *Shangri-La's Rasa Sentosa Resort, Sentosa; Tel. 6275-0100.* Open daily for dinner. Dine under the stars on the white sand beach at Sentosa. Try Sharkey's Seafood Sensation, a wonderful plate of lobster, prawn, scallops, mussels, squid, grilled vegetables, rice and garlic bread. Major credit cards.

The Tandoor $$$–$$$$ *Basement One, Holiday Inn Park View, 11 Cavenagh Road; Tel. 6733-8333.* Open daily for lunch and dinner. One of the city's most highly rated Kashmiri restaurants, the Tandoor is best known for its fresh breads and oven-baked dishes, such as the lobster tandoori. Major credit cards.

Tepak Sireh Restoran $$$ *73 Sultan Gate; Tel: 6396 4373.* This resplendent mustard-coloured building adjacent to the Istana Kampong Gelam was originally built for Malay royalty. Its recipes are reportedly handed down from generations. Only buffet-style meals; recommended are its spicy and tender beef *rendang*, squid curry (*gulai sotong*) and pandan tea.

Top of the M $$$$ *39th Floor, Meritus Mandarin Hotel, 333 Orchard Road; Tel. 6831-6258.* Open daily for lunch and dinner. This revolving restaurant with a magnificent view offers continental choices prepared by French chefs. Major credit cards.

Town Restaurant $$$$ *1 Fullerton Square, Fullerton Hotel, Civic District; Tel. 6877-8128.* Open daily. With windows on the river at historic Cavenagh Bridge, the upscale Town restaurant, off the Fullerton lobby, specializes in a fine Sunday brunch and a varied selection of Asian, Western, Japanese and Mediterranean dishes. Guests can also wine and dine alfresco. Major credit cards.

Vansh $$–$$$$ *01-04 Singapore Indoor Stadium, 2 Stadium Walk; Tel. 6345-4466.* Open daily lunch and dinner. A fine example of New Asian dining, this restaurant near the Kallang river combines a groovy, sexy ambience with modern Indian cuisine. On the menu is a range of tapas, tandoori and teppan-style meals. Major credit cards.